I ho[pe] [you enjoy]
the journey !

♡ Ghislaine

Mastering

Your

Inner World

What others are saying about this book:

"Ghislaine Mahler is a great person and a great coach. In her book *Mastering Your Inner World,* she suggests creative ways of working with archetypes and provides valuable guidance for the self empowerment journey. Bravo!"

Ken Blanchard, coauthor
The One Minute Manager and *The Secret*

"Ghislaine Mahler presents a true road map for personal success from the inside-out. You'll love the Journey!"

T. Harv Eker, author
Secrets of the Millionaire Mind

"The principles Ghislaine Mahler created are very powerful. Apply these principles and watch your life transform!"

David Wood, author
There Is a World in my House

Mastering Your Inner World

Your Doorway to Creating an Empowered Life

Ghislaine Mahler

Copyright © 2006 by Ghislaine Mahler

ISBN 0-7414-3391-5

Orders: www.ghislaine-mahler.com

Mahler, Ghislaine.
Mastering Your Inner World: Your Doorway to Creating an Empowered Life/Ghislaine Mahler
1. Self-actualization (Psychology) 2. Goal (Psychology)
3. Archetype (Psychology) I. Title.

Photos by Joey Jones – www.exposuremax.com

Published by:

1094 New DeHaven Street, Suite 100
West Conshohocken, PA 19428-2713
Info@buybooksontheweb.com
www.buybooksontheweb.com
Toll-free (877) BUY BOOK
Local Phone (610) 941-9999
Fax (610) 941-9959

Printed in the United States of America
Printed on Recycled Paper
Published August 2006

With love, to my mother Hélène who gave me some of the greatest challenges to overcome, challenges which became the most precious lessons I would ever learn.

Contents

Part One – Finding The Hero Within

Part Two – Harnessing Your Dragons

Part Three – Gathering Your Allies

Part IV – Claiming Your Kingdom

Part V – Developing Mastery

About the Author

In the late 1950's, Ghislaine was a little girl growing up just outside of Paris. Her parents had recently purchased their first television. One day a whole new world opened up for Ghislaine when she saw a major theatrical production made for television, with hundreds of actors wearing masks of Warriors from Mesopotamia. From that day, Ghislaine knew that she would be on stage some day; this was her destiny. Little did she know that her passion for the stage and for masks would not take her to the theatrical world, as she had thought at first, but to become one of the leaders in human potential and personal transformation.

Ghislaine studied maskmaking with Cyril Dives, the renowned French artist who had created the masks she had as seen on television years before. She attended acting school at Francois Florent School in Paris and Herbert Bergdorf Studio in New York, studied documentary filmmaking at NYU, and began making masks and props for major Broadway productions, including Cats and Phantom of the Opera.

While Ghislaine loved her involvement in theater, she felt there was more to be done. She moved out West and started teaching the *magical art of maskmaking to students of all ages, from 5 to 85. Mask-making had become for Ghislaine a tool for self-discovery and flowered into a new passion: helping others find their authentic self and step into a new life of possibility and fulfillment.*

For over two decades, Ghislaine has impacted the lives of thousands of men and women from three continents, and has become one of the elite members of the training and coaching profession. She has worked alongside some of the top trainers and coaches in the world and is highly sought after for her unique approach to personal transformation, her special brand of magic and heart. She invites you to join a community of people just like you, who want to find their true mission, and step into lives that are joyful, exciting, successful, and passionate.

Acknowledgments

First I want to thank Spirit for inspiring me to write this book and for giving me the courage it took to get it done. Thank you to my loving husband Stephen for all your support and encouragement. Thank you to my dear friends Georgann, Taren, Lisa, Jamie, Cameron, David, Tom, Michele, Audrey, and Margi for your love and unconditional support to me over the years. Thank you to my wonderful sister Shoju, your love means the world to me. This book would have been a disaster without the precious support and help of my new friend Barbara who shared with me her editing skills. So, to you Barbara, my deepest thanks, and also thank you David and Stephen for your excellent suggestions. I also want to thank Mark and Shawn for giving me such enthusiastic feedback when I took the risk to use my masks in front of an audience of professional coaches. You gave me the confirmation that being fully true to myself was powerful and right. I want to thank you, T. Harv Eker for trusting me to work with your workshop participants, and for being such a powerful teacher for me. Finally, I want to thank Oprah Winfrey for being such an amazing power of example for me, and ... oh, yes! Thank you in advance for having me as a guest on your show. I hope it happens soon. I also want to thank all the wonderful men and women who have given me their trust by becoming my clients. Finally, I want to thank each and every one of you, my readers. I wrote this book for you. May it be meaningful to you and guide you at some point of your Journey.

May your path be blessed and filled with wonder and magic.

Introduction

The concept of Mastering Your Inner World™ came to me gradually as the result of intensive personal work over the past twenty years. Also, I received many teaching gifts from my coaching clients as we explored their Inner World together. They responded powerfully to the exercises I had been creating and their progress accelerated dramatically. I have now decided to trust my inner guidance and make these ideas accessible to many more people with the writing of this book.

When I started understanding clearly that my mission in life was to work with people to create better lives for themselves, I thought psychotherapy was going to be the vehicle for my work. Just at that time, the new and exciting life coaching profession was taking off. Like many others in the mid-90's, I was unaware of this dynamic field for transformation. Once I realized the dramatic results that were possible through the coaching relationship, I knew I had discovered my path. The focus of the work was on creating a future rather than on healing the past. That corresponded to the stage of development I was in at the time. I had done years of psychotherapy myself, and was ready for the next phase: creating a life from a place of passion, integrity, love, and fulfillment-- creating a life from a place of choice.

I started my professional coaching training at Coach University, opened my practice and started working with clients. At the time, I was living in Santa Fe, New Mexico, and many of my clients, adults in personal or professional transition, wanted to make changes to come closer to their vision of a happy, fulfilled life.

In my early twenties, I had studied the art of theatrical mask making with Cyril Dives, a renowned artisan mask maker in Paris, and throughout my life, I had continued to work on masks. When living in New York, I had contributed my art to many theatrical productions, on and off Broadway, ballet performances, advertising, commercials, etc. In the following years, I had moved out West and started teaching this magical art form which had greatly added to my personal discovery and growth over the years. Often, I witnessed my students going through a similar enlightening and powerful process of self-discovery and transformation while making their masks. The masks they were creating represented hidden, deeper parts of themselves. I had left the theatrical world to continue exploring the world of personal growth, and it eventually dawned on me that the mask making and the coaching venues of my work could be put together.

Over the past few years, my mask making work started taking a different turn. My creations were not so much expressions of emotions, but more expressions of different energy patterns within me. Gradually my masks helped me get in touch with different facets of my Inner World. I started dialoguing with these different parts of myself and developing conscious relationships with them. I quickly realized that this approach enabled me to become very intentional with my thoughts. This process was very empowering and helped me to transform much more rapidly and powerfully than I had been able to before. I started using similar concepts with my clients, and they too were able to make rapid and profound changes.

With this book, I am passing on to you what has been given to me through my creative journey. I know if you apply what you read, you will get results beyond what you thought possible. The techniques are powerful and will enable you to eliminate what has blocked you in the past and what is holding you back now. It will require work, persistence, and a willingness to change on your part, and in the end, you will find it is well worth it.

Who would have thought the shy, insecure and lost young woman I was, would turn out to be the powerful and fulfilled person I am today?

My friends, let me tell you that if I can do it, so can you. We are so generously gifted with the power of choice. What will you choose today? Are you willing to do what it takes to build an empowered and fulfilled life for yourself?

If you are, I want to welcome you. I invite you to join me in the Inner World circle and to dance with me towards an extraordinary life.

You Are Not Alone

You Are Not Alone

I remember a comment my mother made to me many years ago. I am not certain how old I was, maybe in my late teens or my early twenties. I never forgot what she said: "In life, we are alone, always alone."

My understanding of what she meant then was that we may have family members, friends, husbands or wives, partners or companions. However, in the end we are alone because nobody can do our inner work for us. That is true, of course.

However I have a different philosophy about this: Indeed, we are not alone! Let me explain: When we think of ourselves, as human beings, we think we are a whole being, just one, altogether being. One person, one mind, one heart. It is true and it is untrue. There are many facets to us, many parts with different thought patterns, different energy patterns, different value systems, different beliefs and outlooks on life, different goals and agendas. Let's be totally clear that I am not talking about a multiple personality disorder. Rather I am introducing a new level of awareness about ourselves.

You may be experiencing some reaction by now, and I will ask you to just keep on reading and trust this wonderful process. I invite you to search within yourself, and learn about new ways to relate to yourself and your Inner World. Indeed, there are many facets to who we are. Some parts within us are in conflict with each other, causing us to experience confusion, lack of clarity, blocking our ability to grow or attain our goals. Part of the work I have done with some of my clients has been to help them get in touch with these different parts and to enter in conscious relationships with them. By making clear agreements with the sometimes warring parts of themselves, they are able to create amazingly rapid results to resolve issues they had unsuccessfully worked on for years.

When doing this inner work, change happens fast. We gain control of our lives, we master our emotions and our thoughts; we develop more harmonious relationships, with ourselves first and then with others.

Rather than sharing from the academic world of research, the wisdom I have gathered and now teach to others has come from my own deep learning and experience. I have always had the ability to be in touch with my inner knowing, my inner guidance, and my intuition. Many lessons have been passed on to me this way. The knowledge I am now passing on to you developed slowly and gradually within me, a mix of bits and pieces that eventually all fit together. As I became ready, it came to make sense to me.

I will share how each of these parts revealed themselves to me, although they will not necessarily be presented in the chronological order in which I discovered them. Instead, I am presenting them to you in an order that hopefully makes sense and supports your growth and development. Some of these parts may already be familiar to you; some others may be somewhat new for you to consider and engage with.

Exercises

With each part, I will suggest exercises and techniques to maximize the benefits of your efforts. Believe me, they will be well worth the work. Some of you will just read the book through and never look at it again. Others among you may decide to work slowly over several weeks or months, and let yourselves develop your awareness in a deep way. Some of you will want to explore together and will join in our community through our Mentorship Program or our Seminars. I encourage working at your own pace, and honoring yourselves enough to listen fully to what each part has to say and wants to do. As you know, books and tapes don't work if YOU don't do the work. Reading a book is one thing, doing the work suggested is another.

Along the way, I will relate stories and examples. Sometimes they will be coming from my personal life, sometimes from some of my clients'. The names used have been changed to protect their privacy.

Four Categories of "Beings"

There are four major categories of "beings" within us, presented in this book:

1. The Self-Esteem Robbers, such as the Inner-Critic and the Inner-Judge. These bring us down. They minimize who we are and what we do. They want us to stay small, and never change and grow.

2. The Self-Esteem Boosters, such as the Inner-Warrior, the Inner-Teacher, and the Inner-Lover. These are our allies. They want us to grow and succeed.

3. The Board of Advisors brings wisdom and creativity to us. They are the Inner-Teacher and the Inner-Magician, the guides on our Journey.

4. The Leadership-Circle is where we find the Inner-Queen and Inner-King. They take us to the next level of mastery in our lives, when we become ready to guide others.

Finally, we will learn how to put it all together, to make our lives fulfilling and joyful, to become the master of our universe.

About Gender

Throughout this book, I alternately use masculine or feminine gender when describing our different parts. My choice is not sex stereotype related. Rather it feels to me as a feminine or masculine energy. Please understand that this is MY experience, and that yours may be different. I may connect to some of these inner-parts differently than you would. For example, my Inner-Critic feels very masculine; however, some of my clients feel their Inner-Critic as a feminine part. So, all along, please do adapt the gender to what feels right for you.

As I close this chapter, I feel excitement for you, knowing you are embarking on a fascinating adventure.

Enjoy the journey!

Part One

Finding
The Hero Within

The Inner-Hero

The Inner-Hero

We all are heroes. Many of us don't know that, but we truly are. Look at children and watch them play. See how they do know they are heroes. In my children classes, I have seen boys play with their swords, defending themselves against imaginary dragons; and most girls dream of being princesses, in search of their prince and their castle. They see themselves as the heroines of their imaginary tales.

Raising our children and reading fairy tales to them is part of our culture. We generally do not think past the fact that it is fun to enable our children to dream

Remember, when you were a child? What did you dream about? What were your imaginary tales? Did you know then how invincible you are? Did you know then that anything you set your mind to was possible? As children, we do not think in terms of possible or impossible. Things just are; dreams just are part of who we are; we express ourselves fully and put action into that full expression.

Then we go to school, and we are asked to start "fitting" into a box that most often does not resemble who we truly are; the box takes on the form of what others' expectations are for us. That wondrous sense of self starts to get fuzzy, confused, and we gradually lose ourselves. If we are lucky, a remarkable teacher crosses our path and helps us recognize and nurture that wondrous rich spirit within us. Few of us, unfortunately have had that experience. Some of us had parents who were determined to have a doctor or a lawyer in their family. Who we were was not nurtured. Our journey was strongly influenced by parents or teachers or even dictated to us. There it was -- that box which we knew wasn't ours. But we were told it was, and somehow it became really difficult or even impossible to say "no." They made it look so good, so appealing.

When I was a child, I developed a passion for theater, and my dream was to become a professional actress and tour my beautiful country of France with a theatrical group. My mother decided otherwise and I ended up at age fifteen in a technical college, learning stenography and typing. That was my mother's box, not mine. I was not permitted to even discuss whether or not I wanted that box. It was imposed on me. By then, I was so afraid of my mother that I couldn't find the strength to stand up against her will. This was a long detour on my journey. However, this obstacle created an opportunity for me to learn how to say "no" to what was not in harmony with my spirit. This became a long battle. It took me many years to become self-confident and strong enough to find my own voice. I am here to tell you that it is never too late.

Adversity is a Gift

I have no regrets. The adversity I encountered in the early years of my life is the gift that challenged me to seek my Inner-Hero. Isn't this what the journey of the Hero is all about? Isn't it what life is all about? Each day, we encounter challenges which we turn into problems or opportunities, depending on our character. I have often wondered why some people are blessed with courage and passion, while others seem to lack the energy necessary to continue forging their own path. Being a hero takes courage and determination.

It is often in adversity that we learn. I have encountered people who grew up having everything and anything they wanted, and life was too easy for them; the lack of challenge turned them into "softies." They were depressed and bored. Their Inner-Hero had never been challenged to fight for what they wanted. They were lost. This reminds me of the story of the butterfly, which you may have already heard. Before becoming a butterfly, the pupa is in its cocoon, growing slowly. Eventually it transforms and grows wings, and it is soon ready to break the cocoon, come out and fly away! If you decide to "help" the butterfly and break the cocoon open too soon, it comes out and dies. The butterfly needs to develop strength in its wings, and the way it does that is by working on opening the cocoon.

Parenting is one of the hardest jobs there is. It is often difficult to know where to draw the line between being indulgent, making it too easy for children, and being too harsh or demanding on them to the point that it damages their self-esteem. It is also difficult for many to know the difference between encouraging children to develop into who they are versus who mothers and fathers want them to be. Whatever the circumstances of our childhood have been, we must look at our lives today as a wonderful opportunity to forge our character and strengthen our wings.

Do you look at your circumstances as opportunities, or do you choose to turn them into excuses?

What has your hero's journey been? What are the big lessons you learned? Do you look at your circumstances as opportunities, or do you choose to turn them into excuses to avoid making a positive decision, or just give in to laziness, and give up on life?

A Hero doesn't say: "Oh well, I guess I will go fight the ogre tomorrow. For now, I want to watch TV." I wonder if you are smiling in recognition that this anti hero attitude might at times be yours. I know it is sometimes mine, perhaps more than I want to admit to myself. Sadly, some of us stay home to watch television. We watch others live lives of passion on a square screen rather than doing the acting ourselves. We never start on our journey. Have you at times given up on life? Have you given up on your dreams and aspirations? Have you given up on yourself, abandoned your Hero within?

I know there is still a flicker of light within you, or you wouldn't be reading this right now. It is time to take this flicker of light into your hands, time to return to the Hero or Heroine within you. It is time to say YES to your life, YES to your dreams. It is time to voice your true heart's desires and live your life with passion and determination.

We all come here with a mission. What is yours? What journey will your Hero or Heroine embark on? It is all up to you. Life is full of exciting possibilities. Grab onto them!

Learning in Action

Think of someone who is a Hero or Heroine to you and answer the following questions:

- What are the inherent qualities of this person?

- What makes them a hero? Write a thorough list of these qualities, attributes that make them unique and heroic to you.

- Where are these qualities and attributes in you?

- How can you nurture and grow these qualities in yourself?

- What outlets can you create today to express and bring to life these qualities?

Continue journaling about this until you have achieved a new level of clarity about your Hero or Heroine within. Take three actions each day to express your heroic qualities.

The Inner-Child

The Inner-Child

In the mid-eighties, I lived in New York City and started working with a psychotherapist. I was lucky because I was referred to a person who had done her own personal work, and helped me get to the core of things rather rapidly. The core for me was to work with and heal my Inner-Child. At the time, John Bradshaw was instrumental in this trend with his book *Healing the Shame that Binds You* which I have since recommended to many of my coaching clients. If you are familiar with John Bradshaw's work, you know how critical it is to heal the child within. I feel so much gratitude toward him and the legacy he shared with us all. Without him, I may not be here today to share what I have to share. Sounds dramatic? Well it's true.

My therapist in New York advised me to start working with one of her partners, in a therapy group. I will never forget the first time we got acquainted with our Inner-Child. Peter guided us through a visualization exercise, inviting us to find our Inner-Child - *There she was, little Ghislaine, maybe three or four years old, so cute with her blond braids, but she was very unhappy. In fact, she was frightened! My mother was angry and yelling at her. My little girl was crying, desperately looking at me, the adult Ghislaine, and imploring me with her eyes to remove her from my mother's abusive grip. I was looking at the scene, frozen, totally incapable of moving toward them. I was absolutely paralyzed.*

I came out of the visualization mortified with feelings of shame and guilt. I didn't know how to rescue my little girl. I felt so badly, because I knew how painful it was for my little girl to stay there. I didn't quite realize at the time that not only was this part of my past, but it was also very much part of my present. This was the experience I was re-enacting internally; this was the relationship I had with that part of myself, that child inside, who was in such pain! I remember sharing with the group what that experience was. My memory of the rest of what went on in the group that day is blurry, but I do remember quite clearly what happened for me afterwards. I made a firm commitment to myself and to my little girl, inside, that I was going to do whatever was in my power to change myself so I could take care of her.

So, every day, as advised by Peter, I went to visit my little girl, right there inside my consciousness. In the morning, I would go and look for her, and every night, before going to sleep, I would go visit her again. At first, it was difficult to find her. Sometimes she would be hiding; sometimes I would find her in a dark corner, terrified and in tremendous pain. I would just sit there with her. After a while I told her how sorry I was that I couldn't have been there for her earlier. Up until then, I hadn't known how to care for her. I was now in the process of learning. I told her that no matter what, from now on, I would show up every day, and would never leave her again.

I continued visiting her every day; week after week; month after month. Gradually, she started trusting me a little bit more. She would let me hold her, rock her, and sing to her. Little by little, she started opening up and talking to me. I (the adult) became very good at listening to her, listening to her pain, and she cried and cried, for a long time. And then, came one day when there was no more sadness, no more tears to shed. We started laughing together, and she started getting hopeful, and eventually even excited about going out to play.

I remember when I explained to the therapy group one day, that my mother had never allowed me to have a Barbie doll. All my friends at school had Barbie dolls, and I couldn't! My mother had decided that they were improper for young girls because their bodies were developed with breasts. And that was the end of that, no discussion! I remembered how painful that was for me at the time. I had many dolls, but they were all baby dolls, and I really wanted a Barbie doll. Of course, looking back, I understand that it wasn't so much about the Barbie dolls themselves. It was about my desperate need to develop a sense of belonging. It was about sharing with my friends. It was about saying YES to the world, rather than saying NO, as my mother had. That night, after I left group therapy, I drove to the store. I mentally took my little girl with me, and there we went, little Ghislaine and I, on a mission to buy a Barbie doll. She was so excited!

At the store, there was another woman in the Barbie doll aisle. She was there with her two-year old daughter. But I could tell the mother was much more interested in the Barbie dolls than the little girl was. That woman and I had fun together as we looked at all the different Barbies, with their beautiful outfits. My (inner) little girl was just so happy! We chose one of the blondes, wearing red corduroy shorts, a navy blue and white striped shirt, and sexy black boots. We took her home, with a couple of additional outfits, and started playing with her. To this day, I keep that Barbie doll on my bookshelf, because she symbolizes a turning point in my life. My little girl had always been told "NO." This was the moment when I started saying YES to her, inside me.

Wounds that are not healed affect our lives in the present.

This was for me the beginning of a long journey to heal my little girl who had been through so much. Her wounds were very deep. Many of us carry a wounded child inside, and do not realize how wounds that are not healed affect our lives in the present. If that is the case for you -- if you were abused as a child, whether it be physically, sexually, or emotionally, I recommend that you find a therapist who will help you with your family of origin issues. Give yourself the gift of healing your Inner-Child! It is the key to your finding joy and happiness in your life.

For those of you who were not victims of abuse, the exercise at the end of this chapter will give you a starting place to develop a more ·conscious relationship with your Inner-Child. I find that so many people ignore that vital part of themselves. They say: "Oh, that's the past; there is nothing I can do about that." What happened then still affects your present. Your past will continue to do so until you decide to address the difficulties you are having with your Inner-Child and change how you relate to that part of yourself.

The Inner-Child connects us to our ability to dream, to play, to laugh. We live with so much stress these days. Playing and laughing are vital to our ability to create balance within ourselves. With my coaching clients, from time to time, we focus on the Inner-Child. We all need to keep that connection alive, where our innocence, our joy, our excitement reside.

When we were children, we were read wonderful fairy tales and we dreamt, seeing all that was possible for us to create and enjoy during our lives. As we grew up, our circumstances started altering our ability to dream; we could no longer see what seemed possible: education, parental rules, having to fit into a square box, having to be "realistic," all acted on us to change and shape our perspective and values. Our childlike intuition that helped guide us and inform us that our world was boundless and open to new discoveries began to wither. "Lives don't get built on dreams," they say. Life circumstances may have brought some of us poverty, disappointment, and disillusionment.

Dream, children, dream!

That beautiful gem, our ability to dream, gets tarnished over time and buffing it will bring it back to life. Dream, children, dream! Children are connected to their Spirit. Don't we always notice that about babies? The light in their eyes makes us smile because in these eyes we see our "home," so bright and beautiful! Dream, children, dream!

If your Inner-Child has lost the ability to dream and smile, do start the following exercise, and never stop!

Learning in Action

Each morning and every night, when in bed, silently look for your Inner-Child. Sit at her side and notice what she is feeling. Is she talking to you? Engage in a dialogue with her, focusing essentially on listening to her. If you find it difficult to find her, see yourself driving or walking to the house or apartment where you grew up. See yourself opening the door, entering and looking for yourself as a child – maybe he or she is in the kitchen, in the bedroom, or in the living room. Look until you find your Inner-Child. Then, sit there and let the meditation take its course.

The important thing here is to not pretend being anything other than who you are as an adult. It is crucial that your Inner-Child gets to trust you and eventually open up. When I started this process, I had to apologize to my Inner-Child for not having been there for her. Wherever you are in your process, just tell the truth.

See this as a beautiful journey of love – you are entering into a new relationship – you are entering a child's life, a child who really needs you to listen, love, play, understand, and be supportive.

The Inner-Adolescent

The Inner-Adolescent

After spending many years taking in an enormous amount of information and knowledge imposed on us by the adult world, we become adolescents and start affirming who we are. We begin to think in our unique way, about what we actually want and to make decisions that may impact our lives for many years to come. It can be a frustrating time for adolescents as well as for their siblings and their parents. Many parents have difficulty with this stage of development because they have to gently let go of their control and let their children make the mistakes they need to make in order to learn. Parents commonly want their children to "benefit" from their experience and wisdom. But as the butterfly needs to work its way out of its cocoon to grow strong wings, so must adolescents learn for themselves.

It is frustrating for the adolescent whose parents won't let go. To grow into strong, creative, intelligent adults, teenagers must not only be permitted but encouraged to voice their ideas. It is then that they will learn step by step to take full charge of their lives; to take responsibility for their choices. Are you treating young people around you like little children who need to be told every step, every action to take?

My adolescence was a tremendously difficult and painful period of my life. I was never given permission to be who I was. Nor was I allowed to own my aspirations and desires. I was not allowed to go where I wanted to go, do the things I wanted to do, wear the clothes I wanted to wear, nor have the friends I liked. Needless to say, I was not allowed to choose the direction of my life. In this process, I gradually learned to drown the voice of my inner-teenager. It's taken me many years to recover that part of myself.

I became quite sensitive to this and I came to realize how powerful it was to allow my Inner-Adolescent to become more curious, express her ideas, talk about her aspirations and dreams.

People sometimes tell me:

"Oh, you are from Paris? I would love to go to Paris!" And then they look at me resigned to the fact that their desire is just a pipe dream. So, I always respond:

"Oh, that's great, when are you going?" They look at me flabbergasted:

"What do you mean, when am I going?"

"Well you just said you'd love to go to Paris. So when are you going?"

"Oh ... well ... I don't know, I haven't given this any serious thought."

"You haven't? Do you know that when you said you'd love to go to Paris, your whole face lit up?

"Really? Well … maybe I should look into this."

Yes, please, do look into it, whatever "it" is. Don't squash your Inner-Teenager and his or her aspirations. Life is happening now, not yesterday, and not tomorrow. Do something spontaneous, even if it feels totally "irresponsible," allow yourself to act on your desire for freedom and excitement! Go take that dancing class you have talked about for the past fifteen years. Make the time for yourself. Start breaking out of your cocoon and let your wings open wide! I know, you may not feel ready to jump out of your comfort zone, and that's okay. Just start with the little risky things. These are the practice steps that will enable you to know what it feels like later on, when you become ready for the BIG things. If you are not able to take the small steps, how will you ever continue on your journey? NEVER!

Don't squash your Inner-Teenager and his or her aspirations.

For many years, I was thinking and feeling at the deepest core of my being that life and its pleasures were for everybody else. I was not allowed to participate. It was very painful and I felt quite lonely in that place. As I continued on my journey of self-discovery, I started practicing daily meditation and journaling. Here is what happened for me, the day I met my Inner-Adolescent:

There was this special place I would regularly go to in my meditations: *I would jump into a lake, swim deeper and deeper, down through caves and passages, until I could see a light above me – I would now swim upward toward the light, and come out of the water in a different world. I would find myself sitting in the bed of a brook. I would stand up and walk out of the water, to the edge of a wooded area, a beautiful, calm and serene place. Sometimes I would sit under a tree; sometimes I would fall asleep on a mossy bed. Sometimes I would be greeted by a group of elves and dwarves. They always celebrated me, dressed me with beautiful translucent robes, took me by the hand and led me into their village. One day, they ushered me and my little girl to the center of their gathering place. I was now greeted by hundreds of beings who were all celebrating me and my little girl. They were playing trumpets and drums, singing, and applauding us! There were colorful banners and flowers everywhere. My little girl and I started walking up the small hill that was in front of us. In our hearts dwelt a deep sense of ceremony. Once we arrived at the hill top, we turned to face the cheering crowd and they suddenly became silent.*

I knew something important was about to happen but I didn't know what. Within just a few more seconds, I saw a silhouette, someone starting to walk up the hill, towards us. I couldn't tell who it was. After another minute or so, I started distinguishing a young woman. She was very pretty, and full of youth. Most attractive was the life energy she carried and the lightness of her step. As she continued walking up the hill and approaching us, I now recognized her: she was my teenager. Her eagerness and her vibrant beauty were so evident! I had never seen her that way before. She now stood in front of me. I let go of my little girl's hand and reached inside my beautiful silk coat, into a deep pocket. To my astonishment, my hand came out holding a couple of dozen paint brushes. I handed them to my teenager and said: "Go, Ghislaine. Go out in the world, and discover your destiny. Go express your beauty – I now let you go." She thanked me, said goodbye to me and my little girl; she turned around and walked away. Her heart was filled with grace and joy, as she skipped toward a world full of wonderful possibilities."

I had finally given my Inner-Adolescent permission to go out in the world.

After coming out of the meditation, I realized that this was a momentous experience for me. With this meditation I had finally given my Inner-Adolescent permission to go out in the world, to trust who she was and what she felt. At last she was free to express herself fully. After many years of feeling restricted in my life and in the world, I now knew that the world was open to me. Anything was possible for me to do and be.

The next day I signed up for painting classes and started exploring a new direction in my life; a new path on my journey. This was a path that said YES to me, YES to my desires, YES to my expression, whatever that might be. We were now three on the journey, Me the Heroine, my little girl, and my adolescent.

Bob, one of my clients, recently got re-acquainted with his Inner-Adolescent. He had been badly abused by an uncle. His parents, instead of standing up for him and confronting the uncle about his destructive action, chose to brush it all off. They swept the matter under the rug, and never mentioned it again. Bob, an adolescent at the time, learned to deeply distrust his parents. As an adult, he came to realize that because of that situation with his parents, he was unable to this day to have experiences where people really stood up for him. He had developed a tendency to do too much for others, to be too nice, and to feel undeserving of anyone doing anything special for him. During our work, he got to learn to stand up for his Inner-Adolescent. He started asking his wife and friends to stand up for him, and to do special things for him.

Bob realized that he would continue having trouble in his relationships, as long as he was unable to care for his Inner-Adolescent. He had to become willing to stand up for himself. Then, and only then, would he "know" what it felt like to have someone stand up for him. He was then able to reproduce that in his life, in his relationships.

Learning in Action

In the next few days, think about your Inner-Adolescent. You may choose to journal about what your experience was like during your adolescence. Were your parents supportive and did they encourage you to express yourself fully? Did they encourage you to be yourself or did you have to "rebel" in order to be yourself and affirm your ideas and desires?

What happened to your adolescent feelings as you became an adult? Did you abandon them? Did you imprison them into a box that said "no" to your creativity and your passion?

What do you need to do today to re-connect or to connect more fully with your Inner-Adolescent?

Take three actions this week! Make a decision to commit to your Inner-Adolescent and give her permission to be in full expression. How will she fully express herself?

The Inner-Parents

The Inner-Parents

Separating from our parents is a normal stage of development as we are growing up. Depending on whether our emotional needs were met along the way by our parents, separation happens in varying degrees and at different times with each of our parents. Many experts have written about this subject. Here, I will not write about the different needs and phases of normal development from a research perspective. What I will relate however, is my own experience with that process of separation and the effect it has had on my life.

The Inner-Mother

I was at a Twelve-Step convention in upstate New York, the first time I consciously realized how much I was still internalizing my mother's sternness and beliefs. The second night of the event was an evening of celebration and dance. Everyone there would be clean and sober, and we would dance into the wee hours of the night. After struggling with my usual self-doubts about my looks, I remember clearly making a powerful decision: I wasn't going to care what other people might think about me. I was going to have a great time and dance, dance, dance!

I did dance, and what fun I had! The next morning I got up around 6:30 and jumped into the shower to get ready for the meditation meeting at 7:00 a.m. I turned the water on, and right then it came: my mother's voice. "How dare you have so much fun last night? Who do you think you are?" The voice was so loud in my head, I couldn't believe it. Wow! Fortunately I was beginning to develop enough awareness to detach from that voice and not let it shame me. I knew that voice that was speaking wasn't ME. I could have recognized it in the largest crowd. It was my mother's voice, with all her negativity, shame, coldness and control. I remember saying to myself: "Yes, I had fun last night, and I am glad I did. Leave me alone."

I started really paying attention to my thoughts. Was my internalized mother always talking to me?

After that incident, I started really paying attention to my thoughts. Was my internalized mother always talking to me? Even before I had developed other beliefs or rules to replace hers, I started the process of saying NO to my Inner-Mother. It didn't matter if I felt bereft of direction and left with no knowledge of what to do. This was the process of separation I needed to go through, a process which I had never been able to go through before. To that day, I had not realized that I was still abiding by the rules my mother had imposed on me during my childhood. I had to first become aware of that before I could change it. It took a while. I remember becoming very angry; I had to release all the anger pent up in me towards my mother for holding me back; anger towards myself for having allowed that for so long. I felt safe, finally able to say NO to my internalized rules and regulations which had never been mine in the first place.

Work with Your Inner-Mother First

As I was changing in this way, I became terrified of hurting my real mother. However, I realized that my internal work would soon enable me to be a more loving person to my real mother. At last, I wouldn't be in inner conflict with her. I was able to become angry at my Inner-Mother and separate that from my real-life mother.

A few months later, I went back to France on vacation. I picked up my parents at their home near Paris and drove them down to one of my sisters' home in the beautiful south of France. I did have to put my foot down with my mother during the few days I spent with her. Because I was no longer tolerating my Inner-Mother's sternness and negativity, the contrast with my real-life mother started becoming evident. How could I continue to tolerate my real-life mother's constant belittling and criticism of me? I had to make it very clear to my mother that I would no longer tolerate her negativity. It was time she learned to appreciate rather than criticize me. I was able to make a clear and firm request. I didn't raise my voice. I was calm and firm. She was quite shocked when it happened because it was unexpected and it certainly was a new behavior on my part. It took her two days to accept the new me. When I left a few days later, she hugged me for the first time ever. Since that day, my real-life mother has always treated me with the utmost respect, and we have since developed a relationship based on love and acceptance. Looking back, I feel very proud of the journey she and I have shared. It was difficult, but how passionate and how rewarding. Today she is eighty-nine years old. I know we have done our work together. She knows I love her, I know she loves me. This is much, much more than I ever thought we would accomplish on our journey together.

My Inner-Mother has become a soft, warm, unconditionally loving part of myself. She is a majestic Queen; a Goddess who supports me always.

---

*The way we relate to our Inner-Mother
is directly related to the way
we treat our Inner-Child.*

The way we relate to our Inner-Mother is directly related to the way we treat our Inner-Child. Looking at this aspect of ourselves is so important. It eventually all comes together like pieces of the puzzle. It also shows up in our outer life. If we have children, we often see ourselves doing exactly the things with them that our mother did with us. Yes, we find ourselves engaged in the behaviors we swore we would never repeat. Why? Because we haven't come to terms with our differences with our own mother. Where we need to put our attention to find healing and resolution is mostly inside of us. This is where the power is ours to change. Once we change inside, the outer circumstances are easy to rectify.

Learning in Action

What relationship do you have with your Inner-Mother? Is she loving, supportive, nurturing? Spend a few days reflecting and/or journaling about your Inner-Mother. Do you need to make some changes in this relationship? What do you need from your Inner-Mother?

Make a list of the qualities you want in your relationship with your Inner-Mother. See what is already there, and what is not. What can you do today to improve that part of your inner world?

The Inner-Father

With the Inner-Mother, we look for unconditional love, nurturing, and support. With the Inner-Father we look for strength and to be provided for. There lies the foundation for our ability to be successful financially and in our work.

If you grew up in a single-parent family, it is possible that you have not developed an inner-parent of the missing gender. If that is the case, you may choose to reflect on that, evaluate what is missing for you, which of your parenting needs weren't met. You may also decide to go on a Journey to create an Inner-Mother or Inner-Father, currently missing in your inner world.

Here again, it is from my personal experience that I will speak. My father was a good man, loving and courageous. Struck with polio when he was a young boy, he nevertheless led a normal life. Although he experienced a lot of physical pain throughout all his years, not once did we hear him complain about it.

I adored my father; he was my hero. Unlike with my mother, I felt safe with him. During my adult years, and more particularly during the years I was in therapy, I began to realize that my father had never really stood up for me in the face of my mother's abuse. I now understand that my father did not know what to do. What became important for me to understand was that I didn't have the experience of an Inner-Father who would stand strong, and show up for me. I realized that I didn't have a father who would provide for me emotionally. So guess what kind of relationships I created in my life? I attracted either men who would be controlling and abusive like my mother, or men who would be emotionally shut down and hide, just like my father.

Part of finding my Inner-Father involved a period during which I became angry and resentful of my real-life father.

I started searching for my Inner-Father. During this process, I realized that no matter how much he loved me, my real-life father had been unable to stand up for me in the face of my mother's abuse. How could he have not done anything when he heard me scream from the upstairs bathroom? Every Sunday was the ritual of washing my hair. Every Sunday I was terrified of the same thing happening again: my mother, tired, angry and frustrated, would force my face under the running faucet as I sat naked in the empty tub. I would cry and scream, gasping for air, in utter terror. She would proceed by slapping me and yell: "There! Now you have a reason to cry!" She would then continue pushing my face under the water. I was the youngest of six children and they would all be downstairs with my father. Not once did anyone come up to my rescue. Once finished, my mother and I would come downstairs. She would shame me and proclaim what a bad girl I had been, once again. They would all remain silent. She was the ruler and my father was unable to challenge that.

I went on a journey to find an Inner-Father who was really there for me.

So, in time, I went on an inner journey to find an Inner-Father who was really there for me. I started watching Bill Cosby on television, in his role of the father in "The Bill Cosby Show." It was amazing for me to see how he was able to talk to his children and his wife, making himself vulnerable about his imperfections. I continued my research of father examples everywhere I went. During all this time, I kept telling my Inner-Father that I wanted him to stand up for me, to be strong, and to face his fears. I told him that if he wasn't going to change, he could no longer be my Inner-Father. Sadly, it didn't work. I guess that particular Inner-Father was a lost cause. His habits were too strong to be changed. I decided to fire him and go find another one. This was a new concept for me. I didn't know I could fire one of my inner-beings! After all, why not? This was MY Inner-World, and I ought to be able to do whatever I pleased with it!

On my search for a new Inner-Father, I made a decision to "discover" what men were really like. I remember, flying back from Greece on a jet plane and creating a new plan. I was going to make "friends" with men. That would be my first step. Soon after that, I started a new relationship with a man who would often get together with his male friends. I was living in Colorado at the time. I would sit with them and listen as they would read poetry to each other, play with their swords and act out their heroic stories. They showed me their strength; they showed me their hearts. It was then that I found my new Inner-Father. He is here within me, always, both strong and able to keep his heart wide open. He believes in me and in my success as he advocates for me and loves me unconditionally. My new inner father can be vulnerable and lets me lean against him when I want to. He also gives me a gentle push when I need one.

Learning in Action

Go within and find your Inner-Father. Does he resemble your real-life father? What kind of relationship do the two of you have? Is it the same as the relationship you have or had with your real-life father?

Do you get what you need from your Inner-Father? What do you need? What do you want from him?

Make a list of the qualities you want in your relationship with your Inner-Father. See what is already there, and what is not. What can you do today to improve that part of your inner-Self?

Remember, you are in charge of your inner world. It is up to you. Be mindful not to transfer the responsibility onto your real-life father. You are now an adult – you give to yourself what you need.

You give to yourself what you need.

You give to yourself what you need.

You give to yourself what you need.

Part Two

Harnessing Your Dragons

The Inner-Critic

The Inner-Critic

We all have an Inner-Critic. Some of us have developed enough self-confidence in life to be able to keep our Inner-Critic under control. In some cases, we learn to transform him into an inner ally. How do we create this transformation? The Inner-Critic becomes the inner critique, our ally. He reminds us to make certain we are doing our best, becoming a mechanism connected to a value of excellence.

My professional coaching experience has shown me that many of us let our Inner-Critic control our lives in quite a powerful way. An added challenge is that many of us do not have any awareness of the critic's presence. So, what is the Inner-Critic?

It is a voice inside us who speaks down to us and is disempowering.

It is a voice inside us who speaks down to us and is disempowering. This voice may start small, discouraging us from taking small steps, but if we leave it unchallenged, it grows to dominate us and our lives. My Inner-Critic sounds like this: "Oh, Ghislaine, who the hell do you think you are for wanting to be successful in life? You are writing a book? Nobody is interested in what you have to say, they'll think you are an idiot! Success is not for you; it is for others, but not for you. Just get it through your head. How many times am I going to have to tell you this?" - Sounds familiar? This voice lies to us day in and day out, and we believe it, most of the time. In fact, many of us go through life not even realizing that we are following the voice of the Inner-Critic twenty-four hours a day, seven days a week. That voice never takes time off. We may just think that this is who we are. What a lie that is! Believe me, this is just a trap into which our Inner-Critic has put us.

Why do we do that? There may be several reasons:

- Listening to our Inner-Critic enables us to remain in our comfort zone. No risk taken, no failure.

- We may experience a deep lack of self-esteem, as we feel internalized shame about who we are. If we didn't get the appropriate healthy mirroring of our sense of self from the caretakers who raised us, we grow to feel inadequate.

- We get into the habit of believing what others say, like "you have to work very hard to succeed." These are just beliefs taught to us about life in general, and we bought the concept. If we haven't done so already, now is our opportunity to question our beliefs and make our own decisions about what we believe to be true about and for ourselves.

In his book "The Four Agreements," Don Miguel Ruiz talks about *the domestication process* we all go through during our childhood. I could not agree more. Remember what it feels like to look into a baby's eyes? Do you know how much those eyes shine? What is that? That light is pure love and joy, and we know they are so close to their true essence that they can see ours as well. Gradually as parents impose their views, their beliefs, and their values onto their children, the true essence of their children diminishes and eventually vanishes. The fire in their eyes diminishes. Depending on the degree of love they fail to receive, sometimes that fire transforms into fear, anger or depression. Sometimes it turns into self-destructive behavior or even violence. If we grow up with a parent, caretaker, or a teacher who is too critical, we start internalizing a self-critical dialogue. Sadly, we often continue buying into it for our entire lives. As children, if an adult tells us we are bad, not good enough, we believe they are right and we start internalizing a new sense of self. Right? That is indeed what happens, but it is the process that is defective, not the children. What a child learns is a simple reflection of the adults' sense of self, not that of their own.

---

*What a child learns is a simple reflection
of the adults' sense of self,
not that of their own.*

Understandably, this creates huge problems – people let go of their true inner dreams and their true nature. They get into careers that have nothing to do with their desires, their passions and their authentic selves. As an adolescent, I was forced by my parents to go into a career direction which was directly 180 degrees opposite to what I wanted: I was meant to work in the theatrical world, on stage, and travel from city to city to perform. Instead of going to theatrical school, my parents made me go to a technical college to get office skills. I know to this day my mother thinks it was a better choice for me. Well, that was just her vision, not mine. She thinks she did something good by that, but the truth is that this buried my ability to dream, to believe in myself, and it took me close to twenty years to finally break free from working in an office. Twenty years!

Sam – Unwanted Stepchild

When Sam, one of my coaching clients, came to me, he wanted life coaching to change his career path. He had worked very successfully as a surgeon, which required very delicate and precise movements. Over the years he had developed some major neck and back problems which eventually forced him to stop his work. We started the coaching process, and I quickly realized that Sam was suffering from low self-esteem -- he was dealing with a very powerful Inner-Critic. As a boy, he experienced the pain of rejection everyday with a step-mother who did not want him around. When he came home from school, he could not get into the house because she locked the doors and forced him to wait outside for hours no matter how bad the weather. She was extremely critical of him, and Sam felt rejected and wounded. His deep insecurity prevented him from living the life he truly wanted.

As an adult, Sam had come to surgery almost by accident. As we continued the coaching process, I learned that Sam truly wanted to be an artist and was unable to give himself permission to pursue his dream. His Inner-Critic had him in chains. As soon as I encouraged Sam to voice his Inner-Critic and to challenge that part of himself, he took charge of his life and was able to make great changes. As a matter of fact, he expressed his desire to learn maskmaking. He became my apprentice for over a year, and by the time we stopped working together, Sam was a true artist. He had found a new voice within himself that encouraged and approved of him.

Entering into a Conscious Relationship with your Inner-Critic

I recommend giving your Inner-Critic a name, so it becomes easier to dialogue with him. Do not choose the name of one of your parents, because it is important to separate your Inner-Critic from your mother or father. Remember, as an adult, it is your responsibility to handle your inner conflicts, and not to use this work as an opportunity to blame your parents. Pointing your finger and blaming the outside is a diversion from your own inner work. It can simply be a way to be in denial, and to carry yourself as a victim. What is offered here is an opportunity to empower yourself and your life, and become happier and much more fulfilled by learning how to deal with your Inner-Critic.

Here is an example of how entering into a conscious relationship with your Inner-Critic can transform you. Bob is an upper-level manager in a large corporation. It is his first year in this position and he has been very focused on making his job a success. In this way, he has succeeded. However, he has been spending many hours at work and has had less time than he would have wished to dedicate to his family. He has missed precious time with his young children in particular. Next Wednesday morning is an award ceremony at one of his sons' school, and Bob really would like to attend and be supportive of his boy. But he is struggling with the fact that he will have to take the morning off work. Here is how his mind works:

Unconscious Dialogue:

Inner-Critic (IC): Oh, forget about taking the morning off. You should be ashamed of yourself. How can you even be thinking about that? The kids will be okay. After all, their mother will be there with them. You should be at work no matter what.

Bob: Wow, you're right! There is no way I can miss going to work tomorrow morning. There are all those emails waiting to be responded to. If the people I work with don't get me on the phone, they will have trouble helping their customers. Yes, but my kids really need me too. Oh, I don't know what to do here.

IC: Of course you know what to do! You are going to work! You can go next time with the kids. They are okay. Your job is more important right now. It's your first year, and you have to pay your dues.

Bob: Yes, it's decided. I am not going to take the morning off. I have so much work to do, I would be really overwhelmed if I did. Plus, what is my boss going to think? He is going to think I am starting to slack off ... I really don't want that.

Another possible version is that Bob decides to take the morning off because he really wants to be there for his children, but he will spend the whole morning thinking about the work that is not getting done, and he will feel very guilty. In other words, although he will be there physically, he will be absent emotionally and mentally – unavailable to his children.

As you become more conscious of your Inner-Critic, you will be able to take charge of your inner-dialogue as well. Here is what you may experience then (still using the same example as Bob's):

Conscious Dialogue:

IC: Oh, forget about taking the morning off. You should be ashamed of yourself. How can you even be thinking about that? The kids will be okay, their mother will be there with them, right? You should be at work no matter what.

You: Well, X (name you gave your Inner-Critic), it looks like you really want me to feel guilty about this, huh?

IC: You bet I do! You are supposed to work hard. Taking the morning off -- are you out of your mind?

You: I am not going to feel guilty. It is a good thing for me to take this morning off to be with my kids. This is a special day and I want to be there for them. My work can wait. It will be there for me to do in the afternoon when I get back to the office.

IC: Shame on you! How dare you talk to me like that? You are supposed to listen to me. Imagine what they are going to think about you at work! Nowadays you must give 200% if you don't want to get fired. Come on, forget about that morning off.

You: X, you are not allowed to be part of this decision. Just go away. You will be allowed to speak when you have something constructive to tell me. Any negative comment is not welcome. I am taking the morning off, and that is the end of it.

It is quite possible that your Inner-Critic will not let go very easily. It is by doing this conscious work repeatedly and persistently that the Inner-Critic eventually shrinks, and transforms into an ally. At first, when you start ·challenging your Inner-Critic, you may need to be much more direct and say such things as "go to hell" or "shut up" to your Inner-Critic.

The Inner-Critic will attack your emotional self, but your intellectual self knows what is right for you to do. So, if you find yourself having difficulty making decisions and shutting your Inner-Critic down, you can have recourse to your intellectual knowing; what you want is in alignment with your values and with what is right for you.

In the example above, Bob brought this issue to me during a coaching session, because he was feeling very guilty about taking this half-day off work. He was quite concerned about it. In a prior session, Bob had done some work on discovering his values. I reminded him that his top value was "family." I then encouraged him to voice his Inner-Critic, and it became very clear to him that taking the morning off was the right decision because it honored his top value; it then became a simple matter for Bob to tell his Inner-Critic to "go to hell" and that he was the boss.

Sometimes to prevent you from having to get out of your comfort zone, your Inner-Critic will trick you in a different way. Here is an example of a reverse situation: You must be at a meeting that is really critical for you to attend. One person whose presence makes you feel really uncomfortable will be there. Your Inner-Critic will find all the reasons why you shouldn't go to that meeting. The dialogue could sound like this:

Inner-Critic: You know, it isn't that important for you to go. Look, you have all these emails you need to respond to. If you go to that meeting, you are going to waste two whole days away from the office. Do you know what your in-box is going to look like when you get back? Your daily email flow, what is it ... about 150 emails per day? Look at that! You'll have about 300 emails to read. No way!

The Inner-Critic can be so strong that he truly runs your life. I have had clients admit that they prefer not going on vacation because they know they will have so much work to do when they return. The Inner-Critic loves a corporate culture that supports that kind of thinking.

In your life, what is the role of your Inner-Critic? Who is the boss? Who is in charge? What kind of life do you want to have?

Learning in Action

Exercise #1:

Start being mindful of your inner dialogue. Chances are, you will recognize your Inner-Critic very rapidly. We ALL have one. Sometimes it is very loud; sometimes, it speaks more softly. This exercise is about starting to notice how you deal with your Inner-Critic. Do you let it dictate your decisions? Do you end up feeling angry or envious? Do you do what you want despite your Inner-Critic but find yourself feeling guilty about that?

This first exercise is not about changing anything, but about noticing your natural inclination. In general, what pattern have you developed in dealing with your Inner-Critic?

Once this has become clear, proceed to exercise #2.

Exercise #2:

When you catch yourself listening to your Inner-Critic, stop what you are doing, and take a couple of minutes to focus on your thinking and create a conscious dialogue with your Inner-Critic.

Initially this may be difficult for you. Start by focusing on the intellectual reasoning for what you want. Become clear about the decision that is right for you. Then go back and listen to your Inner-Critic. Respond by confronting what you just heard. For example: "Wow, X, you really seem to want me to feel guilty here. What is this all about?" Then listen to how your IC responds. Do not give in by doing what the IC wants. Just continue the dialogue until you truly understand what your IC is saying. You will be amazed by what you will learn about yourself. Once you have taken in the learning, announce to your Inner-Critic that you are no longer going to let it run your life. From now on YOU are in charge. It is probable that your Inner-Critic will become louder and try to control you even more strongly for a while. Don't be alarmed; this is normal and predictable. Try to just laugh. Your playfulness will disempower and dissolve you Inner-Critic's energy. Be persistent and consistent with this process. Soon, it will become a habit for you.

Over time, when you are in the habit of being in charge, instead of your Inner-Critic, you will start discovering that the inner voice which used to control you and bring you down, is transforming. It will act as a healthy reminder to put your best in everything you do. That voice will become your Inner-Critique, acting as a friend who is an advocate for you.

So keep practicing and know that it will not always be as difficult as it may seem right now.

The Inner-Judge

The Inner Judge

The difference between criticism and judgment can often be subtle. For this reason you may have difficulty differentiating your Inner-Critic from your Inner-Judge. Over time, it will become easier. To criticize is to find fault and point it out. A judgment is a strong opinion.

Having good judgment is considered a valuable quality. It is the process of forming an opinion about someone or something. When it comes to judging, our beliefs and our history will always influence our thinking and thereby our judging. Being judgmental however, is also defined as "characterized by a tendency to judge harshly" whether it be towards ourselves or towards others. There can be sternness with the Judge that is generally not present with the Critic. The Critic blabbers all day, if not kept under tight control, while the Judge is a firm and final voice that is not open for negotiation. The Judge will express definite opinions and often speak in harsh terms such as "You are a stupid person", or "you are a bad person."

The Judge is also a tool we use when looking at others, in order to avoid looking at what is going on internally. For many of us, it is easier to look at friends and co-workers and judge their appearance or their actions, rather than it is to look at ourselves. The Judge loves to flatter our egos by comparing us to others. An example would be: "Wow, look at that man over there! Wow ... he is so fat, I don't understand how someone can let themselves go like that. How disgusting! Thank God, I don't have that problem!" or "These rich people have it so easy! How hard is it to stay in shape when you don't have anything else to worry about? Well, if I had that kind of money, I would certainly look like that!"

It is obvious that this kind of thinking denotes a real problem on the part of the person carrying that Inner-Judge. It is likely that this person is experiencing a struggle about her appearance and is not able to be honest with herself yet. When our Inner-Judge is focusing on others, it is a sure sign of personal denial.

Another version of this process would be someone who uses her Inner-Judge as an ally to carry herself as a victim. For example: "Wow, these rich people -- they have it so easy. How hard is it to stay in shape when you don't have anything else to worry about? Poor me, I have all these other things to do. I have to work all day, and then I have to come home and clean the house and feed the kids. Life isn't fair ... It isn't my fault if I am fat!"

In both cases, there is a lack of taking responsibility. Using the Inner-Judge is a mechanism of personal disempowerment. We are in denial, refuse to take responsibility, and carry ourselves as victims. Obviously, this doesn't work too well, does it? Not only does it not work, it is a waste of precious energy and time. It also causes us emotional pain and sadness, and sometimes even depression. It truly poisons our lives and our relationships with others.

Using the Inner-Judge is a mechanism of personal disempowerment.

The good news is that in the same way that we are not powerless over our Inner-Critic, we are likewise not powerless over our Inner-Judge. The first step is to become aware of our thinking patterns when using the Inner-Judge. One question we might ask ourselves is: how do we form our sentences? Do they start with "you" or "they", like "you are so stupid" or "you said this and that"? If we do, chances are we are functioning from our Inner-Judge. Most likely, we are in denial and refuse to take responsibility.

The second step is to ask ourselves: Okay, what is it I do not want to look at within myself? The answer may not come easily. Right at that moment, the Inner-Judge may charge back and say: "There is nothing wrong with you. It's all about them. Look at them! It's their fault!" The more the emotional charge we feel, the more we can see that we are attempting to stay in denial. Remember that looking inside requires a change, and change can be scary; it is much easier to stay in denial than to break a pattern. Further along, in this book, you will discover some inner allies who will help you. Remember, you are not alone!

The third step is to enter into a conscious dialogue with the Inner-Judge. This could look like this:

You: "Okay, I can see you Mr. Judge! I know you are trying to fool me into believing I have no responsibility for what is happening.

Judge: "You are damn right! This has nothing to do with you. You are great! You did nothing wrong here. Look at them ... they did it!"

You: "Well, that's nice, but I am smarter than you think, and I know that when you get really excited like that, you are trying to take over. I have no desire to let you run the show here. So, I am going to ask you to shut up right now."

Judge: "Look, I know better than you. I am telling you, look at them!"

You: "Very tempting, but no thanks. I know I have a part in this, and I am going to look at that right now. So, please don't interrupt."

As you read the above dialogue, you may be thinking "Wow, this stuff is crazy!" It is not crazy, it's just that you've been hypnotized by you Inner-Judge. He has taken over your thinking. You Inner-Judge is sneaky and will do whatever is needed to keep you disempowered and in denial.

Remember, the other side of the Judge is a gift. Having good judgment is valuable. If we do have this innate ability to form an opinion, we can decide to turn this ability into a tool that will always serve us for the better. When we find ourselves being judgmental, there is work at hand. A judgment is a reaction to something triggered within ourselves, a button being pushed, something we do not want to bring to light. So, if we want to grow, we choose to look inward and discover what is really going on. Can you see how our Judge can become a real friend by giving us these opportunities to improve ourselves?

It is not easy to say "no" to our Inner-Judge. Sometimes it can feel really good to wallow in judgment. However, it doesn't need to last very long, or we may drown in bitterness, resentment, jealousy, and envy; or we may even indulge in gossip, which is nothing other than two or more people engaging in conversations with their Inner-Judges together. If jealousy or envy is what you are feeling, it is better to acknowledge that feeling, rather than reacting to it by gossiping, which spreads our poison in a very damaging way. Working with our Inner-Judge can be difficult at first, but it is possible. Make a firm commitment to a 100% no-gossip rule – it is a good place to start. It is a conscious choice we have to make all the time. We are either in the problem or in the solution. We either choose to grow or we accept less from life than we deserve, and over time our spirituality can die. Challenging the Inner-Judge requires a lot of work, but the rewards are great. Once you start the process, the chances are you won't want to stop. You will feel so clear and empowered. Remember that judgmental thinking is like poison; it is toxic, and takes us away from our creativity and our personal power.

So, let's get started, shall we?

Learning in Action

Get a note pad small enough to carry with you all the time. For several days, write down every instance where you catch yourself thinking from the Inner-Judge. These thoughts are the "You ..." or "they ..." sentences and they are thoughts that are minimizing and disparaging of others.

Once you have a few days-worth of notes, choose a quiet, undisturbed time to read them over and see if a particular issue seems to show itself. Deep inside, you may know what is really going on. Take this opportunity to gather your thoughts around the issue. In which direction do you want to put your focus? If your Inner-Judge starts talking to you, engage it in a dialogue and practice taking control over this issue. You may not be successful at first, but persistence on your part will guarantee your success. Continue practicing this exercise as many times as you may need. Over time, it will get easier and easier and you will become an expert. After a while, having a judgmental thought will feel so strange that it will be effortless to shift right then and there.

Remember, it is a matter of choosing the direction you want for your life: up or down, better or worse, forward or backward, whichever is "right" for you. We are the masters of our inner world, we can always choose.

Light and Dark
We Need it All

Light and Dark – We Need it All

We live in duality – it is everywhere: black and white, yin and yang, left and right, day and night. It is all around us, and it is in us as well.

Mastering our inner world does not mean we completely eliminate the dragons, the negativity, the doubt, the challenges. There will always be more dragons showing up, more challenges to overcome, more negativity to transform. Remember, it is only by entering into the darkness that we can see the light. It is only by facing the dragons in our inner-lives that we can reach our kingdom.

What mastering our inner world means is that at any time, we become more and more efficient at rapidly shifting from the dark to the light. It means that we don't wallow in self-pity and discouragement but swiftly see where we have choice. This is the most empowering moment, when once again, we choose to keep moving to fulfill our vision. We continue growing and expanding beyond our comfort zone, as we are faced with growing challenges. All of this is part of our human experience.

I sometimes see clients who want to "eliminate" the darkness of their Inner-Critic for good. Well, my friends, sorry to disappoint you, but the news is that it will never happen. For the sun to shine in Australia, the moon must shine in

America. In order to truly appreciate the light, we must also come to appreciate the dark for the contrast it offers us. The dark offers us the opportunity to grow and expand so we can move toward the light.

Appreciating the darkness does not mean we must live "in" it or that we will stay stuck there. It means we must be aware of it for the beautiful duality it creates. It is from this awareness that we can see and choose the light.

When your Inner-Critic and Inner-Judge act out, see them as your signals and reminders to step into the positive side, and evaluate the work at hand, wonderful opportunities to grow and learn.

Part Three

Gathering Your Allies

Writing a New Script

Writing a New Script

Are you ready for a new script? Are you ready to let go of your old story, the story that keeps you small and in hiding? Imagine yourself being the director of a brand new play. The best part is that not only do you direct it, but you also are the one writing it! You get to choose all the characters in it, the plot, the outcome, everything! We are such wonderful creators.

Every six months or so, I revisit my life script, check everything in it, and get to adjust, and rewrite any part I want. I can change the ending, the characters, or decide I don't like that play anymore; it may no longer fit who I am as I keep growing. Playing with my new and vibrant script is fun and it keeps me on my toes.

If you haven't ever done so, examine the story you tell yourself and others about yourself. How is that story for you now? Is it challenging you to grow and expand? Are there any missing characters in your cast? Or are there any characters that no longer serve your life purpose? What will you do about that? Is there anything in your story preventing you from being true to yourself?

Remember, you are the Director, and YOU are in charge. It is all up to you. If you start telling yourself "I can't" and get into a self-defeating dialogue, STOP! Take a few minutes to re-center and re-group. Remind yourself that this is part of the old script and shift into the new script. Simple? Yes. Easy? No, because we are beings of habit, and habits take effort to change. Impossible? Absolutely not! Remember, if I can do it, so can you. And I keep reminding myself that if you can do it, so can I.

At this stage of my development, it is no longer an issue of whether or not I can live my life in this new way. It is that I can no longer allow myself not to. Get it?

Thankfully, we have many inner-Allies to help us create a powerful and winning story. These are your new cast members. Enjoy meeting them!

The Inner-Warrior

The Inner-Warrior

When I worked for an employer, I felt secure about my skills and my ability to perform the tasks or projects I was assigned. It was once I decided to go on my own, create a business, and be my own boss that the challenges showed up. My Inner-Critic was having a great time, telling me what a failure I was going to be. But my nature always told me that it was more important for me to do what I loved, no matter how scary, rather than being a "worker among workers." So, I felt that I had no choice. I had to take the risks. I didn't know how to build a business, I was naïve and inexperienced, and my expectations were unrealistic. For many years, I went ahead building my business by trial and error, not knowing that I actually could find the help I needed. What I did have, however, was immense courage and a willingness to work on myself and continue growing regardless of the cost. What I didn't know then, is that I was using my Inner-Warrior to help me get things done.

No matter how inexperienced I was when it came to developing and growing a business, I was determined to follow what I felt was the right direction for me. Since I was not conscious of the "ask for help and support" concept, I had to find the resources I needed within. As a result, I gradually developed awareness of a different energy inside, an energy that was powerful, strong, fearless, determined, and persistent. Wow

... what was that? Feeling this new energy, I went to my art room one day and started working with clay to make a new mask. What came out was a Warrior-Woman. She wore a medieval spiked helmet, adorned at the top by a fierce looking snake.

This was for me a totally new concept, and it felt really good to realize that this energy had been in me all along; I just hadn't been able to feel it before. My Inner-Warrior encouraged me, told me to ignore my Inner-Critic, and assured me that no matter what, she would be there for me. Together we started on our journey.

I recently taught an eight-week maskmaking class with a group of ten children, five girls and five boys. The theme of the class was "Finding the Hero Within." Within the first half-hour of the first class, one of the boys just "got it." "Oh yes!" he said, "the hero, that's the guy inside who is courageous and loyal, and I am going to put him in the mask. Then, I will be able to see him!" Not bad for a 10 year-old. A few weeks later, almost done with making his mask, he put it in front of his face and said: "You can do it, Alex!" It was such a joy for me to see a young child getting the message so clearly. What a powerful concept for him to understand! No matter what the circumstances, he will always be able to tap into his inner hero!

So, yes, the heroic saga of the human race is what we are meant to experience. The Warrior, however, has the distinctive function of "overcoming" or "winning" something, which for me is a better choice of words than "fighting."

Whether it is a war with monsters or foreign armies, or our inner demons, like the Critic or the Judge, there is a sense of overcoming something. For many of us, what we must overcome is our fears and our negative beliefs.

As a woman and as a life coach, I have been blessed to work with many women who initially, hadn't been able to be in touch with their Inner-Warrior. Little girls are told not to be angry; little boys are warned not to cry. So, naturally, it is easier for men to find their Inner-Warrior than it is for women. As a French woman brought up in France, I had the interesting model of Joan of Arc, whom we studied in school. So, as a little girl, I always understood the concept of a woman with a calling, who listens to her inner guidance and valiantly follows her beliefs. The sad part of the story is that people felt threatened by Joan of Arc's Warrior energy. After she vanquished the British and pushed them out of France, the church and the French royalty turned against her. They charged her with being a witch and burned her at the stake. Today, it is more common to see strong women express their Warrior energy and live their passion, but it still makes many people uncomfortable. Yes, we have a lot of progress to make in this area. All of us, men as well as women, need to become more aware of our Warrior energies. What we are talking about is our personal power. We must not be afraid of expressing our personal power. Furthermore, I believe we ought to help each other find and express that beautiful, vibrant part of ourselves.

*We ought to help each other
find and express that beautiful,
vibrant part of ourselves.*

There are many different types of Warrior energies. I will present three of them here.

The Great Warrior

The first one, which so many of us are trying to identify with, is what I call the Great Warrior. She is the one who takes the actions she needs to take, even when she is afraid; she is unstoppable and walks triumphantly toward her conquest. This Warrior has no need to be violent, but her energy is focused and her intention is clear. No matter what the obstacles are along the way, she does not loose track of her vision and her mission. She never falters and she never gives up. She is beautiful and stands tall. She is a great leader. Her mind is always focused on the results she wants to achieve. She knows who she is and she is fully confident of her upcoming success.

The Wounded Warrior

Another kind of warrior is the Wounded Warrior. That Warrior is also courageous and persistent. However, he is not fighting to go toward but to walk away from something. This

Warrior is a survivor. I discovered my Wounded Warrior while working on my second Warrior mask. I was still very much in touch with that vibrant energy inside me, and decided to make another Warrior mask. He was beautiful; wearing a Gaelic helmet with bull horns! I was almost finished working on the clay design when I suddenly felt him talking to me and saying: "Cut my upper lip, cut my upper lip."

I followed my inner guidance and started working the clay by just using the energy coming through my hands. To my utmost surprise, there he was, my glorious Warrior with a cleft lip! I was completely baffled ... what was that about? I knew it felt right, but I couldn't' figure out why he had to appear so wounded. There was the key word; he was my wounded Warrior, the one who had had to overcome some major obstacles. He was the one who had to run for his life to save me from abuse and addiction. He was such a courageous Warrior, and he had definitely won my battles. Yet, he was so sad and so tired. There he was with his deep blue eyes looking straight at me. I couldn't figure out why his eyes were so intensely blue, since mine are brown. A couple of years later, I sold this mask to a young man who had participated in a workshop with me. I presented some of my work and he so related to the wounded Warrior that he had to buy the mask. The young man had a set of deep blue eyes ... just like the mask. Sometimes, I just wonder.

The Fierce Warrior

The third kind of Warrior is the Fierce Warrior. This one has built a thick armor around his heart. He appears fierce and tirelessly keeps fighting, no matter what is happening around him. I had a client recently who showed me that warrior. Mary and I were working during a coaching session, and she was talking to me about her relationship with her supervisor at work. "I hate it when I have to lose! I present him with my ideas and he refuses them; he wins, and I hate to lose." The tone of Mary's voice was quite elevated, and I asked her to explain what she meant with her choice of words such as "win and lose", like being on a battlefield. We explored that further, and soon discovered that she was indeed carrying herself as a Warrior who was constantly at war. That's how she perceived her life to be.

The Fierce Warrior is a Wounded Warrior who has developed a strong defense and does not feel safe showing his wounds. He feels so threatened that everything around him seems like a danger or a threat. He believes there's something to fight against, even when there is no danger anywhere near.

Which Warrior do you relate to the most? To some extent, many of us relate to all three Warriors. Depending on the amount of personal work we have done on ourselves, we will relate to one Warrior more than the other two. In certain situations, when we feel in danger, it is crucial to tap into the Fierce Warrior energy because we do indeed have to protect ourselves. However, problems will arise if we use the Fierce Warrior energy too often. Remember, it is fear that motivates the Fierce Warrior to action; she is being reactive, not pro-active; she is defensive, not responsive. That behavior can cause difficulty in our relationships by gradually isolating us in both our outer and our inner lives. We become more and more disconnected from our true Self.

Relating to the Wounded Warrior too closely may result in our walking around like a victim. We have probably all attended a social event and somehow gotten "hooked" by a victim. You know what that is like: someone starts a monologue about her distress, and how terrible her life is. As you try to disengage, she will tell you more than you want to hear about all her troubles. Believe me, it takes a Great Warrior to walk away, because she can be quite persistent and follow you. Have you ever caught yourself being that victim person? We all have, to varying degrees of course. So, when we find ourselves complaining, whining, or justifying our circumstances, we are behaving as a victim. That brings poison to every cell of our body. That poison kills; it kills our dreams, our vision and our intention, and it saps our energy. It is also very contagious. It contaminates people around us, and it can spread like wild fire. When you catch yourself in that frame of mind, it would be wise to make an immediate readjustment before too much damage has been done. Or, if you find yourself in the company of a victim, someone who blames, whines, and complains, ask yourself what you are doing there. Chances are you'll catch this person's poison. The voice of the victim can be quite insidious. I recently realized that I was so much in the "not wanting to be a victim" in my life, that I was using someone else's being a victim as a situation that felt victimizing to me! Once I got over the shock of my new realization, I had to admit that my Wounded Warrior is still a part I identify with, even though my Great Warrior is very active in my life. Ask yourself: "With whom do I surround myself? Wounded Warriors? Fierce Warriors? Great Warriors?" What kind of mirror is that for you and for your life?

So, like many other things in life, balance is the key. And awareness is the key. Let's do some exercises about that.

Learning in Action

Exercise 1: Think about one situation where you had to gather all your courage to accomplish something which was a scary thing for you to do. What happened inside? Where did you go in your mind? Did you give in to your fear and run away? Did you somehow tell yourself "yes, I am scared, but I know I can do it"? Did you wait until the last possible minute or did you just jump in? Take a few minutes and write down the event. How did you feel? Now, try to remember the mental process you went through. Which warrior did you use?

Exercise 2: (While reading this exercise, please adapt the gender which feels right for you.) Close your eyes and ask your Great Warrior to reveal himself to you. Can you see him? Can you feel a particular energy in your body? When you find your Great Warrior, walk toward him and welcome him. Thank him for all the times he has helped you, encouraged you, and done for you what you needed in the moment. Tell him that you would like to be in closer contact with him than you have been up until now. Listen to what he says. He might start telling you how wonderful you are, and how happy he feels to be with you. You may hear him say that he has always been there for you and always will be. Allow yourself to believe him and embrace what he says!

Over time, as you continue improving your conscious relationship with your Inner-Warrior, make some clear agreements with him, celebrate and thank him. When in difficult situations, always tap into him. The more conscious you become of your Great Inner-Warrior, the easier it will be to keep him close to you as you move through your life.

The Inner-Lover

The Inner-Lover

We are gifted with the wonderful capacity to love. We are born with it. However, many things impact our willingness and our ability to express the love that flows through our hearts.

The environment we grew up in molds the values we have. The environment we create for ourselves as adults includes our workplace, our home, and our friends. It includes the goals we set for ourselves, our family, our hobbies, and more. Unfortunately, many of us create an environment that does not truly match our values. Think about this for a minute. Isn't "Love" a value we all cherish? We all want and need to be loved, and we all need to love; it is our source of fulfillment. If we do not let it flow through us, we start shriveling like old potatoes.

What happened right after 9/11? This terrible day suddenly changed our environment and demanded something more out of us. People came together and poured love from their communal hearts. They reached out to help in every way they could. We all loved what that felt like because this is who we are meant to be; this is what we are meant to express. But gradually, within the next few months, the old environment that we had created for ourselves regained its power bit by bit and most of us returned to our old ways.

Our Inner-Lover is always there, within us, but we do not always let that part of us come to life. We vary in our relationship to our Inner-Lover. Some of us are completely out of touch with her. Some of us are out of touch with other vital parts of ourselves and let our Inner-Lover be so prevalent that we put ourselves in unsafe situations. Some of us are afraid of our Inner-Lover. Some of us think expressing our Inner-Lover is a sign of weakness. Some of us think expressing love is about sacrifice. Some of us learn that sometimes we must practice "tough-love," in order to truly love.

Where is your Inner-Lover? Is she an integral part of your daily life? Are you conscious of her presence? Do you know how and when to let her loose? Could you improve in this area? Probably, we all could, and that includes me, of course.

Love Your Self First

It all starts within. Someone said "we can only love others to the degree that we love ourselves." I find this to be true. How could we ever give something we don't have in the first place? Having the desire to love and to give is not the same as loving and giving. We get mixed up sometimes, don't we? And yet, having the desire to love better can be the start of love. It is a matter of honesty. When it comes to love, we cannot lie to ourselves. We can tell ourselves all the stories we want, but the bottom line is what is true and to maintain our integrity, we must be

.true to ourselves. Even if we don't acknowledge it, we always know when we are sacrificing our integrity.

Loving ourselves first, means:

- Loving our Inner-Child, being in conscious daily contact with him, listening to and making certain all his emotional needs are met.

- Respecting our inner integrity at all times. When we sacrifice our integrity, we must do whatever is needed in the moment to get back into alignment and be true to our selves.

- It is doing what we love instead of spending our days in jobs we hate, just to survive.

- It is having the courage to say NO when we need to, even if it means others may not like it.

- Taking responsibility for all our needs and doing whatever it takes to meet them. Loving ourselves is being conscious of our needs and making sure we aren't resenting anyone for failing to "take care" of us. We are adults, and loving ourselves means being responsible for our life.

- It is taking extremely good care of our bodies, exercising, and eating well, sleeping enough, and drinking plenty of water everyday. It is flossing every night, even when we don't feel like it

- It is surrounding ourselves with loving people who treat us with respect, understanding, and who love themselves as well.

- It is creating an environment that supports us and what we value.

- Creating reserves of money, time, space, love, and energy. Having our finances in order and earning more than we need allows us to create a money reserve and have that precious peace of mind and sense of security.

I cannot say enough about the importance of creating time reserves. There is not one of my coaching clients in the past couple of years who hasn't been severely challenged with time management issues. What are we all running after? Is life truly a race? We forget the value of giving ourselves time to enjoy each minute because we are too busy rushing! The good news is that we can do something about this immediately. Create a reserve of time around everything you do. If you have a one-hour meeting at 1:00 p.m., do not plan something at 2:00. Instead, give yourself that half-hour cushion between 2:00 and 2:30 that is designed just for you to check in, to re-center, and to re-group. If, on occasion, it is impossible for you to have the time reserve between tasks, spend a few minutes breathing deeply. It will help. If you plan some time for re-centering and re-grouping after every task, you will be amazed to see how much more effective and happy you will become.

Create a reserve of energy. This goes along with creating the time reserve. When you are in a rush all day, you deplete your energy because you never give your body a chance to recharge. It is like depleting your cell phone battery. If you do not recharge it regularly, you can no longer make or receive calls. Eating the proper food is also helpful. Sugar depletes energy very fast. How loving is it to eat all those cookies or donuts, only to feel exhausted afterward?

Create a reserve of space. Physical space and emotional space are vitally important to our sense of well-being. Make sure to always have the reserves you want in that area. You will breathe better, and will be able to look at everything around you from a healthier point of view.

These are only a few examples of what loving ourselves **first** means. The most important thing to realize is that it is only when our "batteries" are full that we can truly give. Many people have been trained to put their needs last, thereby becoming martyrs who constantly sacrifice their needs for others. They then become resentful that no one is doing the same for them. Giving from an empty reservoir of love, energy, space, or money, does NOT work. Period. This is why creating reserves is so effective and wonderful. From that place you can love and give all you want. Just make sure you keep filling in your reserves as you give.

I can already hear some of you thinking: "Well, that's really naïve, Ghislaine, where are you from? Life doesn't work like that. Come down to the real world, lady!" What is my response to that? It sounds like your Inner-Critic is rearing its punitive head. Remember, when you are challenged to come out of your comfort zone, the Inner-Critic comes charging. He does not want you to change, so do not let him get into the act.

"Okay," you say, "I am going to give it a try. How shall I begin?"

First, dismiss your Inner-Critic and your Inner-Judge. Second, connect with your Inner-Lover who is right here, ready to come and help you love yourself more fully. If you do not know how to start loving yourself, just ask your Inner-Lover. Develop the habit of connecting with your Inner-Lover on a daily basis, the same way that you connect with the other parts of yourself. I have given you some very specific ideas of how to recreate yourself as a person who loves herself/himself first. If it feels really difficult, start with the very small things, and work your way into the bigger ones. What is important is that you get started and bring this self-loving to play.

Love Your Life

Make a decision to fall in love with your life all over again. Are you bored and disillusioned with life? I imagine not entirely or you wouldn't be reading this right now.

There is nothing like seeing someone die a sudden, unexpected death to realize how lucky we are. Life is an amazing gift! This isn't time to just sit and wait, to let it slide, day after day, and to fall deeper and deeper into boredom and depression! Love your life each day to the fullest! Live your life from a place of passion!

Make a contract with your Inner-Lover to help you get re-connected to your passion. Do not let one more day pass without doing what you want the most. Life is happening now, not tomorrow or next year, or when you retire. Be daring and bold!

Let me tell you about my Inner-Lover. She is this fiery, red, bold, vibrant part of me who cannot wait for me to get up in the morning and be in full expression of my passion, my humor, my energy, and my dreams. Some nights, if I haven't gone to bed early enough and I feel tired in the morning, I might push her away ..." oh, leave me alone, I am tired!" So I may waste a very good morning. Now, don't get me wrong, I am not advocating a life of constant doing. I am a firm believer that it is of the utmost importance that we be human beings more than human doings. Do not forget about the importance of taking time to re-center and re-group, but make sure you say YES to a full life, filled with love and passion.

Love What You Have

It is easy to want another toy, another car, another wardrobe, another this-or-that. We are so conditioned to consume more and more. We are often so trapped in that kind of thinking that we can't even take the time to truly love and appreciate what we do have.

I think it was Oprah Winfrey who said: "If you had everything, where would you put it?" The truth is that many of us have so much stuff, that we loose track of the things we truly love. It all gets lost in the crowd. We become surrounded by clutter. It is in our closets, our garages, our bedrooms, and more. Sometimes we accumulate clutter on our bodies. We don't appreciate being healthy and we don't eat properly, we just want more and more of those sweets.

The key is to keep only the things we truly love, and eliminate the rest. This makes us feel wonderful. It gives us a real sense of appreciation for what we have and fills our heart with gratitude. This energy comes back to us in many ways, which I will discuss in the next chapter.

If you feel overwhelmed and can't even think about where to start, hire a professional organizer. They are everywhere now, because so many of us need their help. They are trained to understand your situation, to guide you through the emotional healing involved with eliminating what you don't absolutely love.

The feeling you want to create is to absolutely love everything you have. Nothing less than that is going to do the job.

Love Being Grateful

Where do you focus? Are your eyes and heart filled with having or not having? Is your outlook about having plenty or not enough? Is it about saying yes or no?

An attitude of gratitude is a choice. Many of us have gone through phases in our lives when we have created lists of what we were grateful for. We did that because we were exposed to that kind of thinking, and we thought it was a great thing to do. But then, we soon forgot all about it as we let some business or some negativity creep in again. "Oh yes," we said, "I used to write at least ten things for which I was grateful. That was nice. Yes, I should do that again." And then, it became just a passing thought in our busy day.

Make a commitment to your Inner-Lover that you will check in with her each day. Let her give you all the love in your heart you need each day so you can feel grateful and appreciative of your life. People will be drawn to you, and everything you do will bring you the results you desire. You will become a magnet for more love and appreciation.

Love Being Here and Now

Many of us spend half our lives thinking about our past, and the other half worrying about what is going to happen tomorrow. Result? We are absolutely not present here and now. So, how can we appreciate our lives if we focus on something we cannot change because it has already happened, or something that has not happened yet?

Our Inner-Lover doesn't operate that way. Anytime you catch yourself being in yesterday or tomorrow, bring your focus back to here and now.

Ask your Inner-Lover to remind you and to help you. Give away your fears and worries to your Inner-Lover who, in turn, will pour love and gratitude into your heart.

Loving Others

If you love yourself, it will be impossible for you not to love others. The love in your heart will overflow constantly and spread to people around you. It is inevitable.

I could have spent lots of energy talking about the tendencies that we all have to become self-centered, arrogant, willful, greedy, jealous, etc. There is no need to focus on these areas because if we are focusing on love, the shadow areas will automatically melt away. What I can say, though, is that when we encounter people who are expressing these shadow areas, we are sometimes tempted to feel fear and resentment, or judgment towards them. The most powerful thing we can do with and for them is to pour love from our heart into theirs. Do it, and watch the magic take place. Love is stronger than anything else.

Your Inner-Lover is one of your strongest and richest allies. Make her/him one of your partners in life.

Learning in Action

It is often easier to notice the areas of our life where we are not expressing love, than where we are:

Without judging yourself, start noticing the areas of your life, your environment, and your relationships, where you do or do not feel and/or express love. Become more aware and mindful of your intentions. Start developing a conscious relationship with your Inner-Lover. What does she look like? What does she feel like? Is she in your heart? Or is she in your head, or in your gut?

Make a commitment to journal on a daily basis about your Inner-Lover. Talk to her, develop clear agreements with her, and ask for her help.

The Inner-Teacher

The Inner-Teacher

Sometimes, we have "inklings" It's the "knowing" that doesn't come from our logical, thinking mind. It doesn't come from our rational mind, but from a place at the core of our being.

Ever say: "I knew it!"? For example, something in you tells you that you shouldn't bother to go to an appointment you have, because the person who is supposed to meet you isn't going to show – and you decide to go anyway, and sure enough the person doesn't show? And you say to yourself: "I knew it!" When you had that "knowing," part of you was by-passing your rational mind. On a conscious level, you felt you didn't have the information you needed. Afterward you realized that seemingly without your conscious mind's input, your "inkling" was correct. Inklings are the language of your Inner-Teacher(s). If you believe you are not in touch with your Inner-Teacher(s), here is where you can start.

You will discover a whole new arena of knowledge, right there, from within.

When we have an inkling, our tendency is to brush it off because the rational mind cannot explain it. However, if you choose to start listening and to follow the guidance provided, you will discover a whole new arena of knowledge, right there, from within.

Your Inner-Teacher gives you inklings, and will give you much more, when you start paying attention and listening.

I remember going through a phase of questioning around this issue when I was living in Santa Fe. I realized that some of my friends had famous, outer gurus and other teachers and they were hoping to learn from them. My approach has always been to learn from within instead. I have always felt, and still feel today, that it is good to learn from others. Look, I hope it is helpful to you to be reading this book. I am passing on to you some of my learning, right? Does that mean you must believe and adopt all of my truth as yours?

NO!

My knowledge and experience are just that - MY knowledge and experience. Some parts may be quite useful and appropriate for you, and some may not. So, you must look inward, and consult with your Inner-Teacher who will let you know what is adequate for you to take on. It is okay to have different opinions from others. What it means is that you can compare your truths with others' and reflect on what other people's truths are. However, if you adopt their truths as yours, you will abandon yours. We all come here with our very personal learning and growing to do. And that teaching comes from within, and only from within. With this in mind, when you go and listen to speakers, remember that what they teach or speak of is their personal experience and knowing. You can listen, and can disagree or agree. You can pick and choose what you like and leave the rest. Most importantly, you must measure what "resonates" as true for you and what does not.

I am astounded when I am at seminars or speaking engagements, and watch people just gobbling down everything that is being said as their new truth. Well? Not so fast! Have you taken the time to check in with your Inner-Teacher to see if you are in agreement? Or did you just brush off the red flags flashing in your mind? Are you just blindly taking in everything coming your way from a person of stature or influence? Do you tell yourself: "oh ... I must have been wrong all this time – if he/she says this, who am I? They have so much more experience than I do; look, they are on that stage, not me!"

NO!

What you must do instead is to connect with your Inner-Teacher and check in: "Hmmm ... and what is my knowing about that subject?" Notice that I didn't say 'what do I think about that?' Remember, the Inner-Teacher doesn't speak to you through your mind, but through your inner-knowing.

Connecting to your Inner-Teacher

In the past twenty years, I have been aware of three Teachers in my inner world. The first one was a Greek woman, draped in a white toga; she would stand on the winding path of a rocky mountain, on the edge of a cliff. I would go meet with her there on a daily basis. At the time, I only knew to hate myself and abuse myself with a lot of disempowering thoughts. My Inner-Critic and Inner-Judge were in total control of my life. My Inner-Teacher was wise, kind, loving, and gentle – she always had wonderful words of wisdom and love for me. She taught me self-acceptance and love.

After about a year, she faded away and was quickly replaced by a Tibetan monk. He was always sitting on the ground, in the midst of dozens of other monks in front of a temple. He would invite me to sit there with him and wouldn't talk to me very much. His presence, however, was so calming, and we would chant together for what seemed like hours. His communication to me was in energy and sounds, not in words. He taught me about inner peace and how to be in the present.

My third Inner-Teacher, who has been with me for many years, is an old wise man. I have never seen his face because he wears a long robe with a large hood. I always meet him in a peaceful Japanese garden. There is a beautiful pond there and we sit on a stone bench just in front of the water covered with water lilies. This Teacher and I have long conversations about all kind of things. He is pure wisdom and knowing.

Sometimes, when I go to the garden, he is already there and says: "well, it took you some time to get here." Sometimes I sit there alone and wait for him. He always comes – always.

Please understand that these "visions" are not fantasies or stories I make up out of my head. Finding your Inner-Teacher does not happen through your rational mind. On the contrary, it comes from not-thinking, from creating this non-thinking space, to just let images flow through your awareness. I find it quite useful to write my visions as they come into my awareness, so my mind focuses on writing the words rather than analyzing or judging what I sense.

Believe me when I say that we ALL have an Inner-Teacher (or more than one) whom we can ALL be in touch with. Some of you may be conscious of that and some of you may not. Some of you may be really new to this concept and feel uneasy about it.

If you have done the exercises in the preceding chapters, it will become easy and wonderful to bring your awareness to your Inner-Teacher. Here is how to do it: next time you feel some inkling coming, your mind will probably want to brush it off. When that happens, tell your mind "no". Right then and there, make a decision to accept and follow the inkling, and do what it says. Make a decision to listen to this part of you and say thank you to this "knowing" for being there. Understand that your Inner-Teacher is the provenance of your inklings. When you become more aware of that, you may decide to start "talking" to your Inner-Teacher. If you are a visual and creative person, you may soon have a visual concept of him or her. If you are not visual, just trust that it is okay to feel that magical presence inside you. Gradually, you will make friends with it, and it will reveal itself to you more and more.

We ALL have an Inner-Teacher.
I am inviting you to open your door
and to listen.

We ALL have an Inner-Teacher. I am inviting you to open your door and to listen. You will be amazed at the amount of wisdom and love in you. The key is to follow that voice instead of the voice in your head, which might be that of your Inner-Critic, or your Inner-Mother or Father telling you not to be this or that, or to do this or that. At first, perhaps there will be doubt, fear, denial, and unease. But as you start following the guidance of your Inner-Teacher and see the beautiful teachings this change creates for you, you will relax and enjoy it.

There will be the influence of other people in your life – your friends, your colleagues, your family, the media, and every other influence you are exposed to on a daily basis. The challenge is to create time and space in your life to be able to hear and listen to your Inner-Teacher.

Just do it – your Inner-Teacher knows best what is just the right answer for you. I had a client who had spent her entire life listening to what other people said was best for her. She was rarely able to make any decision on her own. She would obsess day and night – "what should I do? Maybe I should do this, or that?" – then she would call her friends and ask them what they thought she should do. This arduous process would create even more conflict for her because all her friends had different opinions. What a painful way to go about life!

We worked together for a while with this new process, and she eventually found her Inner-Teacher – the one who provided her best counsel. She started relaxing, and set some boundaries with the world around her. Her friends continued wanting to tell her what to do, and it took some time for her to reeducate them. With persistence and courage, she was able to make that profound change, and her life has been permanently changed.

You too can find your Inner-Teacher.

Part IV

Claiming Your Kingdom

The Inner-Magician

The Inner-Magician

A smile comes over my face as soon as I think of my Inner-Magician. The reason is that my Inner-Magician is full of humor and absolutely loves creating magic tricks in my life. He is full of life and laughter, and he knows all the secrets.

This morning, as I was laying in bed, reminding myself that I was going to write about my Inner-Magician today, I suddenly recalled an experience that clearly put me in touch with my ability to manifest what I wanted in life.

I was living in New York City, in the West Village. I love that neighborhood, mostly because it has a European flair, and the pace is calm and peaceful. My home was a street-level, high-ceiling, studio apartment on Horacio Street. Space was limited and as I was sitting there one night, eating my dinner, I suddenly realized that I wanted a different table. I could just imagine it perfectly: it would have to be round, of medium size, on a pedestal-like leg, and I wanted it to have one of those thick butcher-block tops. Yes! I could see it exactly! All I did then was to imagine it with conviction, feeling myself using and enjoying it in the perfect space. Yes! That was exactly what I desired. That was it, I moved on to thinking about other things for the rest of the evening.

The next afternoon, I was coming home from work and decided to stop by the grocery store a couple of blocks away from my home. As I was approaching the store, I had to cross the street. I looked ahead and saw a huge dumpster in front of a building that several men were coming in and out of. My curiosity was really piqued. Shall I admit to you that I actually thought of having a look at what was inside the dumpster? Yes, I did. So, I walked across the street and followed the sidewalk toward the dumpster. And there, what did I see? Standing on its pedestal leg was my butcher-block top table, smack in the middle of the sidewalk, waiting for me! I couldn't believe it! It was perfect, looked brand-new and was exactly how I had imagined it just less than twenty-four hours earlier.

I asked one of the workmen what they were going to do with it. He said I could have it for twenty dollars. I looked in my wallet and had only fourteen dollars. I had to keep a couple of dollars for my subway fare the next morning. I offered him twelve dollars. He agreed, took the money, stuffed it in his pocket, and off I went with my table, to my apartment just two blocks away.

I heard a huge laughter inside me.
It was my Inner-Magician

While I was walking home, still astounded by the absolute miracle that had just happened, I heard a huge laughter inside me. It was my Inner-Magician – he was having a great time! He had created such a great trick and was quite amused with himself. He was teaching me the art of manifestation. He was teaching me some universal laws about energy, intention, and attraction.

He and I have been great friends ever since. Over the years I have learned the workings of his mind – sometimes I am very successful working with him. When I am not, it is not because he fails me, it is because I try to control the situation and do not let my Inner-Magician do his magic.

Have you found your Inner-Magician? If not, it may be time to start looking for him. He works in a very simple way. Imagine what you want him to manifest in your life – imagine with as many details as possible. If it's an object, think of the color, shape, size, weight, texture, smell of it – imagine it being there in your home. Make the space for it exactly where you want it to be. And with passion in every cell of your body, tell your Inner-Magician that this is what your heart desires. The MOST important rule is that, once you have made your request, you MUST completely let go. Do not start speculating about where it is going to come from, who is going to bring it to you, how much it is going to cost, etc. Doing this is making certain your Inner-Magician will not be able to bring it to you because you are trying to control the situation. Just know that it will come, and let go completely. Your work is done. When it comes, receive with gratitude, joy, excitement, and celebrate!

When you want to manifest a situation such as creating money, being hired for a new job, or perhaps locating an old friend, you can apply the same principles. Get together with your Inner-Magician and tell him exactly what you want. Experience what it will feel like with all your senses. See yourself putting that check in the bank, or working at your new job, or embracing your old friend. Do everything you can to really feel the experience in every cell of your body. Practice this with intensity, just for a half-minute or so, and then let it go completely. It will come. Dance with your Inner-Magician in celebration of the upcoming manifestation.

When you feel ready, start asking for the bigger things you want to manifest in your life. Go for your BIG dreams! If (or should I say: when) your Inner-Critic comes in, wanting to doubt you and your ability to manifest what you want in your life, just thank him for sharing, and move on. Do not give into him and his negative thinking. If you focus on the negative, you will attract more negative. If you need to, go back to the Inner-Critic chapter and read over the part that will help you reinforce your knowing. See your Inner-Critic as a reminder to move from the dark space of negativity, into the realm of wonderful possibility your Inner-Magician offers you.

If you have never consciously worked with your Inner-Magician in the past, I suggest that you start with manifesting small things. Your biggest obstacle, if you let it, will be your mind. Just let go, and move on with the task at hand. Allow yourself to be surprised and delighted when it comes. The reason some of us have difficulty with this principle is its simplicity. This is why using the concept of the Inner-Magician is helpful – it makes it tangible and fun.

Go out and play with your Inner-Magician. Together, you will create all the tricks you want. Have fun!

The Inner-Queen/King

The Inner Queen/King

Your Hero's destination is near. You have walked down the path of your journey. You have harnessed all the dragons coming your way, you have gathered all your allies, and you are now approaching the kingdom. This is the kingdom you have manifested with your Inner-Magician. Can you see your kingdom? The castle is standing right in front of you.

Time has come to find the King or the Queen in you. You must stand as the leader who rules his or her kingdom. When I think about that part of me, I feel myself becoming very tall and majestic. And as I stand there, up on the highest turret of my castle, I know that time has come for me to share my kingdom with the world. I look out to the horizon. My vision is large and wide. I see thousands upon thousands of people reclaiming their lives, mastering their inner-world and creating extraordinary, empowered lives. They are reclaiming their lives from a place of choice, freedom, love, and peace. And as they find their Inner-King or Queen, they too stand majestically, rallying thousands of men and women around them. They too live their life missions to the fullest. They too stand tall, strong, powerful. Their inner-light shines throughout their kingdom and effortlessly attracts others.

The Inner-King rules from the heart. A kingdom created out of greed, fear, insecurity, or anger will generate destruction. It saddens me to see that it is often only in the face of catastrophic events that many of us get in touch with our hearts. Your Inner-King and Inner-Queen come from the heart, always. They passionately proclaim their mission and vision. Can you imagine true leaders never proclaiming the value of their vision to their followers? Can you imagine Martin Luther King, Gandhi, or John F. Kennedy staying home, instead of giving their powerful speeches to the world? How can a vision be manifested if it is not communicated? How can the leader in you, your Inner-King or Queen lead others, if there is no one to follow?

It takes courage to face the world, proclaim your vision, and step into your life mission. Yet, it is then that the world responds, doors open effortlessly and your life truly begins. It is then that you embark on a new journey, **The Journey.** After years of playing small, suddenly you can step into a much larger game. It is then that your life can explode into magnificent fireworks.

Become the King or Queen you were destined to be. Walk the mission you came here to accomplish. At the end of your Journey, when it comes time to close your eyes and slide into another dimension, you will feel joy and deep contentment. You will experience happiness for a mission accomplished – instead of regrets and sorrow for not having lived your most extraordinary life.

Part V

Developing Mastery

You Are the Master

You Are the Master

You are the master of your Inner-World. It is all up to you now, to create your life as you wish it to be. You now have developed a new way to relate to your life, to yourself, to your inner-world. Your relationship to the world is now empowered to the fullest, and it is time to put it all into action. We are beings of habits and it will take some effort to change the habits that do not serve you. You will encounter many obstacles along the way, and you will relentlessly need to face them, and work through or around them. After a while, you will build the muscles you need and it will become easier to catch yourself in a negative habit. You will know it's the time to re-center and correct the direction of your thinking

---

Your feelings will let you know whether or not you are on the right track.

Your feelings will let you know whether or not you are on the right track. Feeling angry, resentful? Maybe you are having a conversation with your Inner-Judge? Feeling insecure or afraid, or maybe just confused? This could be the work of your Inner-Critic. So, be mindful of your feelings; they will act as a barometer of your thoughts. If you find yourself feeling good, you know that you are doing well. Notice that also, and check if you are in conversation with one of your inner allies. Are you in a listening mode and learning from your Inner-Teacher? Are you feeling love for yourself or someone else, maybe for your pet? Your Inner-Lover is dancing with your thoughts.

Connect to your inner world daily

It all starts with your thoughts. Here are a few examples of things you can do on a regular basis:

- As you wake up in the morning, connect with your Inner-Hero and contemplate your day.

- Embrace your Inner-Child before falling asleep at night and tell her that you love her.

- You may choose to go into a morning meditation which will enable you to listen to your Inner-Teacher. When coming out of sleep, you are in an alpha-state, which facilitates a connection to your deeper self. The mind is generally still quiet and you can be open to receive insightful and enlightened information about yourself and your life.

- Taking time for yourself is a great way to honor your Inner-Lover. Get in touch with your gratitude for all that you have in your life in this moment. Feel the glow in your heart.

- You may choose to journal for a few minutes. For me, journaling every morning has been a very effective way to tap into my higher wisdom. Whatever works best for you, do it. When your Inner-Critic gives you all the reasons why you shouldn't take the time to do any kind of meditation, journaling or visualizing, nor to connect to your inner world, send him away!

- When your morning reflection is done, you can get up and start focusing on the day ahead, the projects you want to work on. If you feel uneasy or apprehensive about some of the things you have to do, connect with your Inner-Warrior who will supply you with the energy and courage you need in the moment.

- Encourage your Inner-Adolescent to express his ideas and take the little risks to go for what you want.

- You will need your Warrior when you encounter obstacles. When you are fully committed to your mission, you will not take "no" for an answer.

- Trust your inner-guidance and listen daily to your Inner-Teacher. There will be times when you may not feel connected to your inner-guidance and your intuition. That's okay – trust that it will be there when you need it.

- Remember to take your Inner-Child with you, keep dreaming, playing, laughing, and enjoying your journey to the fullest. This will make your voyage much more colorful and fun. However, make sure not to ask your Inner-Child to handle the responsibilities of your adult. The child is meant to be a child, not a grown-up. The child is meant to be loved and cherished, encouraged and nurtured. The child is meant to play and dream.

• Connect to your Inner-Lover when you look at yourself in the mirror as you brush your teeth. Remember to love yourself, and your heart will be overflowing with the love you can share with those around you. You will glow and attract more love to yourself as well.

Committed to your mission, continue connecting daily to your Hero or Heroine, contemplate your destination, walk down the path with your Warrior, listen to your Inner-Teacher(s), manifest opportunities with your Inner-Magician, and triumphantly walk towards your kingdom. Your Inner-King and -Queen are here to celebrate all of your successes, the big ones as well as the tiny ones! If your Inner-Critic has set you up for failure by imposing unrealistic expectations and demanding that you be perfect, it is time for a BIG change.

Develop Success as a New Habit

Create a Success Box. Write yourself a note every night, listing at least five successes you have had during the day. The little ones count too! Keep your notes in your success box, and visit your box any time you feel unsure of yourself. You will begin to perceive yourself as a successful person in the world. You are reading this book, that's a BIG success! Celebrate with your Inner-King and –Queen. Visualize fireworks in your life!

So now, the only thing left to say is: "DO IT!" Give a copy of this book to some of your friends and create a support group. Get together and share your progress. I know it takes courage and determination to change your habits, especially your thinking habits. This is why I am making a special offer to you with this book. For the next two months, you can join me and others just like yourself, who have read this book, to strengthen your learning and your use of the exercises. We will meet on the telephone for one hour twice a month and discuss your wins, your challenges, and exchange anecdotes. We will all continue learning and strengthening our inner world muscles.

As you transform your inner world, your thinking habits will change, you will feel joyous, fulfilled, committed to your success, and it will be easy to take the actions that lead to a fulfilled outer life. Remember, **it all starts inside**.

So join us – together we can do it. And remember: if I can do it, so can you!

Welcome to Mastering Your Inner World!

Register for Your Free Teleclasses

So, you've read the book, now what?

Join Ghislaine Mahler twice a month in a series of 1-hour classes over the telephone.

Each class will focus on a different section of the book. You will be able to share with others your questions, comments, ideas, challenges, and wins. Most importantly, you will get the support you need to implement your learning from *Mastering Your Inner World* in your life.

To register:
go to **www.Ghislaine-Mahler.com**. It is easy and it is free*.

Reference #: If the box below contains a reference number, you must enter it when registering to any of the teleclasses or seminars.

* *Long-distance telephone expenses are not included and will be your responsibility.*

Our Seminars and Services

The next few pages describe the current services Ghislaine Mahler is offering, including seminars, one-on-one and group coaching.

For more information on seminars, coaching, and products, please go to:

www.ghislaine-mahler.com

**or call
888-488-8553**

Discovering Your Hero Within 3-Day Seminar

Everyone has a hero or heroine inside. With Ghislaine as your guide, you can discover The Hero within you, who will show you your life's true purpose.

We all have special gifts and talents that are unique to each one of us, a specific reason we came here, with specific things to accomplish, a mission to fulfill, a clear journey to embark on. It is The Hero within who takes us on our journey. When we are disconnected from our Hero, we are lost in a labyrinth of trials and errors, of little wins and failures, and mostly we run around in circles that get us nowhere. With The Hero on our side, life becomes an adventure worth living.

During this 3-day seminar, you will:

- Discover or re-connect with your life purpose and your mission;
- Know your unique gifts and talents;
- Learn how to make choices that are in alignment with your values and mission;
- Meet and create an alliance with your Hero within;
- Create your Treasure Map
- Get set ... and Go!

By the end of this seminar you will be energized, on track, and passionate about your life. You will go home with a specific plan of action and the tools you need to get started on your Journey. Most importantly, you will be saying YES to yourself and YES to an empowered life!

Harnessing Your Dragons
3-Day Seminar

Things happen in life that can cause us to give up the Journey to Mastery. Successful people know the power of commitment and staying on course. In this seminar, Ghislaine will teach you how you too can eliminate any obstacle and persevere, no matter what. What used to stop you will become of no consequence.

During this 3-day seminar, you will:

- Identify your dragons and face them
- Learn the secrets to successfully protect your Hero from your dragons
- Own the skills to harness any dragon, for the rest of your life
- Create an environment that is supportive of your Journey
- Transform your dragons into sources of wisdom and knowledge

By the end of this seminar, you will have gained all the confidence and acquired the tools you need to eliminate any obstacle on your Journey. As a result, you will create a bigger plan for your life and you will know that, no matter what, nothing will be able to stop you.

Gathering Your Allies
3-Day Seminar

You are not alone. There are many alliances for you to form, many resources (inner and outer) for you to gather, to insure your complete success. What makes a true Hero? What qualities do you need to develop in order to continue moving forward? Who do you need to become to be the person who gets the treasure on your map? Ghislaine provides the answers to these and many other questions to empower you.

During this 3-day seminar, you will:

- Learn how to tap into your personal power at any time
- Develop a Code of Ethics that is uniquely yours
- Create a support system that will never fail you
- Walk triumphantly beyond your fears
- Become a leader, true to your vision

By the end of this seminar, you will unleash the greatness in you, ready to continue on your Journey, focused on your vision, and surrounded by your inner and outer allies.

Claiming Your Kingdom
3-Day Seminar

There is a balance to be found between seeing your vision and taking action, and setting your intention and letting the universe bring you what you are asking for. Without a clear vision and desire, there is no direction. Without actions, there are no results. Without intention, there is no manifestation. So, how do we know when to act and when to let go? Manifesting what you most desire is an art which also requires you to be a master receiver. You must claim your kingdom to receive abundantly.

During this 3-day seminar, you will:

- Learn the secrets to manifesting what you want in your life
- Become masterful at receiving
- Raise your standards of excellence to much higher levels
- Create space for your kingdom to come into your life
- Open yourself to extraordinary success

By the end of this seminar, you will be part of a powerful mastermind group. You will own the key to creating magic in your life, and manifesting all that your heart desires, regardless of any situation or environment.

Living the Path of Mastery 4-Day Retreat

You have found your kingdom and celebration is on order. Yet, just when you think you have accomplished your Journey, a new path opens in front of you. The kingdom is here to be enjoyed fully and it is to be shared with others. You know you want to share your gifts with others, and sometimes new skills are required to do this with grace and joy. What is your relationship to the world? How big is your world? Do you need to expand your vision again? Coming full circle means starting on your new Journey.

During this 4-day retreat, you will:

- Celebrate your successes
- Explore your relationship with the world as the new YOU
- Define clearly how and with whom to share your kingdom
- Master the art of communication and relationship
- Define what a legacy means for your life's work

By the end of this retreat, you will have stepped into the realm of the Masters. You will have a clear understanding of the legacy you want to create, and the path to bring it to the real world. You will be part of an elite group of Masters who continue to support and encourage each other for many years to come.

Coaching Services

Coaching is a partnership with a professional who has your best interest at heart, and is professionally trained to guide and support you in your personal and professional growth. One-on-one coaching is individually customized, to focus on your specific values, needs and desires, and provides you all the support you need on an ongoing basis as you move forward, make changes, and create the results you want in your life.

Coaching groups are also formed on a regular basis with a specific area of focus. Some groups may be geared to financial freedom, relationships, life mission/vision, personal foundation, etc.

For more information on Ghislaine Mahler's coaching services and programs, please visit **www.ghislaine-mahler.com** or call 888-488-8553.

Other Resources

I would like to acknowledge and thank the three very special persons who endorsed my book:

Ken Blanchard

Coauthor of *The One Minute Manager* and *The Secret*
www.KenBlanchard.com

T. Harv Eker

Author of #1New York Times best seller *Secrets of The Millionaire Mind* and master transformational trainer
www.secretsofthemillionairemind.com/a/authenticyou

David Wood

Children's books author and one of North America's top personal development trainers
www.TheresaWorldInMyHouse.com

Thank you Ken, Harv, and David.